Nourish.

NOURISH THE BODY, NOURISH THE SOUL

COPYRIGHT © 2022 BY JACQUELINE BAXLEY, SUZANNE POTTS, AND WILLEMINA BRAZEAL

ALL RIGHTS RESERVED. NO PART OF THIS BOOK MAY BE REPRODUCED OR USED IN ANY MANNER WITHOUT THE PRIOR WRITTEN PERMISSION OF THE COPYRIGHT OWNER, EXCEPT FOR THE USE OF BRIEF QUOTATIONS IN A BOOK REVIEW.

ISBN: 979-8-218-04822-8

LIBRARY OF CONGRESS CONTROL NUMBER: 2021901158

RECIPES: JACQUELINE BAXLEY
DEVOTIONS: SUZANNE POTTS
DESIGNER: WILLEMINA BRAZEAL
CO-DESIGN & ILLUSTRATIONS: CHELSEA CALKINS
FOOD STYLING: JADE MAGNOLIA
PHOTOGRAPHY: DAKOTA LYNN PHOTOGRAPHY
PRINTED IN CHINA

WWW.NOURISHTHECOOKBOOK.COM

"So whether you eat or drink or whatever you do, do it all for the glory of God." -1 Corinthians 10:31

JUST LIKE THE COMPONENTS OF A RECIPE ARE DIFFERENT AND ADD A NEW DIMENSION, SO, TOO, WE ARE COMBINING OUR BEST EFFORTS TO CREATE NOURISH THE BODY, NOURISH THE SOUL. WE ARE THREE WOMEN WHO HAVE COMPLETELY DIFFERENT SKILL SETS EXCITED TO USE THEM FOR THIS FUN PROJECT.

WILLEMINA IS A GRADUATE OF THE FASHION INSTITUTE OF DESIGN AND MERCHANDISING. SHE USED HER SKILLS TO MAKE A COHESIVE PAGE, CHAPTER, THEN BOOK. SHE MANAGES US AND OUR WORDS TO COMPLETE THE GOAL OF UNIFORM PAGES AND THOUGHTS FOR A BEAUTIFUL CREATION.

SUZIE STARTS EACH DAY WITH PRAYER, JOURNALING, AND A VARIETY OF BIBLICAL STUDIES TO GEAR UP FOR THE DAY. HER GIFT TO OUR BOOK IS A DAILY ENCOURAGEMENT SHE HAS FOUND IN THE BIBLE AND SHARES IT WITH ALL OF US.

JACQUE IS A GRADUATE OF THE CULINARY INSTITUTE OF AMERICA (CIA). THE RECIPES SHE SHARES ARE A COLLECTION OF CULINARY TRENDS. WITH THE ADDITION OF TRADITIONAL FAMILY RECIPES, PREPARING AND EATING SHOULD BE FUN, HEALTHY, AND DELICIOUS.

WE MADE OUR OLD COFFEE TIME OUR NEW COLLABORATIVE TIME: WORKING TOGETHER AND EATING TOGETHER. NOW JOIN US FOR KOFFIETIJD!

table of contents

3-4	CRACKER JACKS | ROMANS 12:12
5-6	NORTH CAROLINA PULLED PORK | JOHN 15:5
7-8	EMPANADAS | ROMANS 8:6
9-10	SPINACH SALAD | 1 JOHN 4:11
11-12	CLAM CHOWDER | ROMANS 15:13
13-14	GINGERBREAD MUFFINS | ROMANS 5:8
15-16	ALMOND SALSA | JOHN 16:22
19-20	CHURROS | ROMANS 8:25
21-22	BEER MARINATED TRI TIP | MARK 4:39
23-24	SLOW ROASTED FRENCH DIP SANDWICH | I CORINTHIANS 13:13
25-26	SPANAKOPITA PIE | PHILLIPIANS 4:8
27-28	FRENCH ONION SOUP | 1 PETER 5:8
29-30	ALMOND PASTE | 1 PETER 3:15
31-32	DUTCH PANCAKES | COLOSSIANS 2:6-7
35-36	RACK OF LAMB | ISAIAH 35:10
37-38	CHICKEN STUFFED CREPES | 2 CORINTHIANS 6:6
39-40	CROQUE MONSIEUR | JOHN 15:12
41-42	TEPPANYAKI FRIED RICE | COLOSSIANS 1:10
43-44	DOUBLE SPLIT PEA SOUP | 2 PETER 1:5
45-46	LITTLE GEM DUTCH SALAD | 2 PETER 1:6

47-48	SLOW COOKED STEEL CUT OATS | 2 PETER 1:7
51-52	APPLE PECAN CROISSANT BREAD PUDDING | PSALM 96:11-12
53-54	FAJITA ROLL UPS | PSALM 91:4
55-56	CRISPY PRESSED POTATOES | ISAIAH 11:5
57-58	TIA'S TAQUITOS DE PAPA | 1 CORINTHIANS 10:13
59-60	EUROPEAN HOT CHOCOLATE | LUKE 16:10
61-62	BLOODY MARY SPICE BLEND | ISAIAH 12:2
63-64	HOMEMADE BLOODY MARY COCKTAIL | PSALM 118:29
67-68	QUICHE LORRAINE | 1 CORINTHIANS 15:4
69-70	EASY OVERNIGHT FRIED CHICKEN | PSALM 34:8
71-72	WINTER ROASTED VEGETABLE SALAD | PSALM 46:10
73-74	SPICY YELLOW RICE SALAD WITH KALE AND VEGGIES | PROVERBS 25:28
75-76	PORTOBELLO PAPARADELLA | PSALM 40:1
77-78	ENDIVE AND BRIE SLIDERS | PSALM 27:13-14
79-80	PRIME RIB ROAST | HOSEA 11:4
83-84	SHORTBREAD SUGAR COOKIE | PROVERBS 15:1
85-86	CANDY CANE SHAKE | ZACHARIAH 9:9
87-88	SHEET PAN SPECULAAS | PHILIPPIANS 4:4-5
89-90	PRETZEL BARK | 1 TIMOTHY 6:11-12
91-92	APPLE TART | NUMBERS 6:24-26
95-96	GINGERBREAD GIFT TAG
97-98	POPCORN GARLAND
99-100	SALT DOUGH ORNAMENTS
101-102	DRIED ORANGE GARLAND

day 01

CRACKER JACKS

INGREDIENTS

1/4 C OIL

1 C POPCORN KERNALS

1 C BROWN SUGAR

1/2 C CORN SYRUP

1/2 C BUTTER, MELTED

1 TSP BAKING SODA

1 C PEANUTS

DIRECTIONS

PREPARE A SHEET PAN WITH PARCHMENT PAPER.

ON STOVE TOP, IN DUTCH OVEN POUR OIL THEN POPCORN KERNALS AND COVER WITH LID. TURN ON BURNER TO HIGH HEAT. SHAKE DUTCH OVEN EVERY MINUTE UNTIL POPPING STOPS, AROUND 3-5 MINUTES. SHAKING DUTCH OVEN, MAKE SURE ALL THE KERNALS ARE POPPED. ONCE FINISHED, POUR INTO LARGE BOWL.

IN A 2 QUART GLASS BOWL, COMBINE BROWN SUGAR, CORN SYRUP AND BUTTER. MICROWAVE ON HIGH FOR 3 MINUTES. ADD PEANUTS AND MICROWAVE FOR 3 1/2 MORE MINUTES.

ADD BAKING SODA AND STIR UNTIL CARAMEL IS LIGHT AND FOAMY.

POUR CARAMEL INTO THE LARGE BOWL WITH POPCORN IN IT. STIR UNTIL THE KERNALS ARE WELL COATED.

POUR ONTO PREPARED SHEET PAN AND LET COOL FOR 30 MINUTES.

TO MAKE MOOSE MUNCH, JUST ADD 1 CUP CHOCOLATE CHIPS TO THE BOWL OF POPCORN BEFORE THE CARAMEL IS POURED OVER IT.

"Be joyful in hope, patient in affliction, faithful in prayer."
- Romans 12:12

ROMANS 12:12 IS WRITTEN IN A SECTION OF ROMANS WHERE PAUL TALKS ABOUT HOW TO BEHAVE AND MORE SPECIFICALLY, PERSONAL RESPONSIBILITY. VERSE 12 SAYS "BE JOYFUL IN HOPE, PATIENT IN AFFLICTION, FAITHFUL IN PRAYER." JUST THINK IF WE STARTED A CHAIN OF EVENTS THAT CAUSED JOY, PATIENCE AND FAITHFULNESS TO SPREAD TO THOSE AROUND US. WE WILL BE MUCH MORE EFFECTIVE IN DRAWING OTHERS TO THE LOVE AND FORGIVENESS THAT JESUS OFFERS IF WE EXUDE THESE CHARACTER TRAITS. IN A WORLD CHARACTERIZED BY ANGER, GREED AND DIVISION, OUR SIMPLE ACT OF RESPONDING WITH KINDNESS AND LOVE MAY MAKE ALL THE DIFFERENCE IN SOMEONE'S LIFE. THE RIPPLE EFFECT OF JOYFULNESS, PATIENCE AND FAITHFULNESS MUST BEGIN IN OUR OWN HEARTS.

notes...

_____
_____
_____
_____
_____
_____
_____
_____
_____

day 02

NORTH CAROLINA PULLED PORK

INGREDIENTS

5 LB PORK BUTT, OR PORK SHOULDER

2 TBSP SALT

2 TBSP PEPPER

1 C APPLE CIDER VINEGAR

1 C KETCHUP

1/3 C MOLASSES

1 1/2 TBSP WORCHESTERSHIRE

2 TSP DRY MUSTARD

3 TSP RED PEPPER FLAKES

1 1/2 C ONION, DICED

DIRECTIONS

HEAT OVEN TO 350 DEGREES.

COMBINE SALT AND PEPPER AND RUB MIXTURE OVER WHOLE PORK BUTT. PLACE IN OVEN. ONCE PLACED IN OVEN, LOWER THE OVEN HEAT TO 300 DEGREES AND LET IT ROAST FOR 4 HOURS.

WHILE THE PORK IS ROASTING, MAKE THE SAUCE FOR THE PORK. IN A SAUCEPAN ON MEDIUM HEAT COMBINE: VINEGAR, KETCHUP, MOLASSES, WORCHESTERSHIRE, DRY MUSTARD, RED PEPPER FLAKES AND ONION. BRING TO A BOIL THEN REDUCE TO A SIMMER FOR 10 MINUTES.

AFTER THE PORK IS FINISHED ROASTING, PULL APART AND PLACE ON SHEET PAN. POUR SAUCE OVER PORK AND ROAST 2 HOURS AT 200 DEGREES.

> "I am the vine; you are the branches. If a man remains in Me and I in him, he will bear much fruit; apart from Me you can do nothing." - John 15:5

IN THE FIRST SECTION OF JOHN 15 JESUS TEACHES ABOUT THE VINE AND THE BRANCHES. THE GRAPEVINE IS A PROLIFIC PLANT WITH EVERY VINE BEARING GRAPES. IN ISRAEL GRAPES REPRESENTED FAITHFULNESS IN DOING GOD'S WORK ON EARTH. THE FRUIT OF THE VINE SYMBOLIZED GOD'S GOODNESS TO HIS PEOPLE IN THE PASSOVER MEAL. WHEN JESUS SAYS IN JOHN 15:5 "I AM THE VINE, YOU ARE THE BRANCHES. IF A MAN REMAINS IN ME AND I IN HIM, HE WILL BEAR MUCH FRUIT; APART FROM ME YOU CAN DO NOTHING", HIS LISTENERS WERE AWARE OF THE MEANING BEHIND HIS MESSAGE. MANY OF US TRY TO BE GOOD AND TO DO ENOUGH GOOD THINGS TO BE ACCEPTABLE, BUT JESUS TELLS US THAT THE ONLY WAY TO LIVE A TRULY GOOD LIFE IS TO STAY CLOSE TO HIM. JUST AS A BRANCH ATTACHES ITSELF TO THE VINE, ATTACHING OURSELVES TO JESUS WILL PRODUCE ABUNDANT FRUIT.

notes...

_____

_____

_____

_____

_____

_____

_____

day 03

EMPANADAS

INGREDIENTS

1 PACKAGE PRE MADE PIE CRUSTS, 2 ROLLS

1 LB GROUND BEEF OR GROUND CHICKEN

1 C ONIONS, DICED

7 GARLIC CLOVES, MINCED

1 C CHEDDAR CHEESE, GRATED

SALT AND PEPPER, TO TASTE

1 EGG, BEATEN

DIRECTIONS

HEAT OVEN TO 350 DEGREES.

PREPARE A SHEET PAN WITH OIL OR PARCHMENT PAPER.

IN A MEDIUM PAN, COOK GROUND BEEF UNTIL IT IS BROWNED. ADD ONIONS AND COOK FOR 3 MINUTES. ADD GARLIC AND COOK 2 MORE MINUTES. SEASON TO TASTE AND COOL.

ROLL OUT THE 2 PIE CRUSTS. USE A CIRCLE CUTTER TO MAKE CIRCLES FOR EMPANADAS. YOUR CIRCLE CUTTER CAN BE AROUND 3 TO 4 INCHES.

ON EACH INDIVIDUAL DOUGH CIRCLE, ADD 2 TBSP OF FILLING IN THE MIDDLE AND TOP WITH 1 TBSP OF CHEESE. FOLD IN HALF AND PRESS EDGES DOWN WITH A FORK.

ARRANGE EMPANADAS ON THE SHEET PAN AND BRUSH EGG ON EACH. THIS WILL MAKE YOUR EMPANADA DOUGH SHINY.

BAKE FOR 12-15 MINUTES.

"The mind of the sinful man is death, but the mind controlled by the Spirit is life and peace"
- Romans 8:6

LIFE IN THE SPIRIT. WHAT EXACTLY DOES THIS MEAN? IN ROMANS PAUL TALKS ABOUT OUR NEW LIFE WITH THE INDWELLING HOLY SPIRIT WHICH IS THE SPIRIT OF LIFE AND IS THE POWER BEHIND THE REBIRTH OF EVERY CHRISTIAN. IN VERSES 5-6 PAUL DIVIDES PEOPLE INTO TWO CATEGORIES: THOSE WHO ALLOW THEMSELVES TO BE CONTROLLED BY THEIR SINFUL NATURES AND THOSE WHO FOLLOW THE HOLY SPIRIT. WE WOULD ALL BE IN THE FIRST GROUP IF JESUS HAD NOT OFFERED A WAY OUT. SAYING YES TO JESUS GIVES US BOTH LIFE AND PEACE. A LIFE LIVED BY THE LEADING OF THE HOLY SPIRIT ALLOWS US TO CHOOSE TO CENTER OUR LIFE ON GOD WHO BECOMES OUR NEW MORAL COMPASS FOR LIVING.

notes...

day 04

SPINACH SALAD WITH DRESSING

DRESSING INGREDIENTS

1 C OIL

1/2 C HONEY

1/3 C TOMATO PASTE

1/4 C RICE VINEGAR

2 TSP ONION, GRATED

2 TSP WORCHESTERSHIRE

SALAD INGREDIENTS

8 C SPINACH

2 EGGS, HARD BOILED

4 STRIPS BACON, COOKED

DIRECTIONS

MIX ALL OF THE DRESSING INGREDIENTS TOGETHER AND WARM 2 MINUTES ON MEDIUM HEAT.

IN A LARGE BOWL, ADD SPINACH. SALT AND PEPPER THE GREENS. TOSS WITH DRESSING.

CHOP THE EGGS AND BACON INTO BITE SIZE PIECES AND GARNISH THE SALAD.

OPTIONAL GARNISHES: CROUTONS, RED ONION, BLUE CHEESE, PEAR, PARMESAN AND MUSHROOMS.

"Dear friends, since God so loved us, we also ought to love one another." - 1 John 4:11

WE USE THE WORDS LOVE AND HATE VERY LIBERALLY IN OUR CULTURE. MANY OF US SAY WE LOVE THIS OR HATE THAT FROM INANIMATE OBJECTS TO PEOPLE. IN 1 JOHN 4, JOHN TELLS WHAT TRUE, SACRIFICIAL LOVE LOOKS LIKE. HE TELLS US THAT GOD IS LOVE AND VERSE 10 SAYS "THIS IS LOVE, NOT THAT WE LOVED GOD, BUT THAT HE LOVED US" AND VERSE 11 GOES ON TO SAY, "SINCE GOD SO LOVED US WE OUGHT TO LOVE ONE ANOTHER". THIS IS AMAZING, CRAZY LOVE! GOD SOUGHT US, LOVES US AND PROVIDES FOR US IN THE GIFT OF JESUS. JESUS IS THE PERFECT EXPRESSION OF GOD IN HUMAN FORM, AND HE HAS REVEALED GOD TO US. WHEN WE LOVE ONE ANOTHER, THE INVISIBLE GOD REVEALS HIMSELF TO OTHERS THROUGH US AND HIS LOVE IS MADE COMPLETE. LOVING OTHERS IS THE PERFECT EXPRESSION OF GOD'S LOVE.

notes...

day 05

CLAM CHOWDER

INGREDIENTS

1/4 C BUTTER

3 SLICES OF BACON, CUT INTO 1 INCH PIECES

1 C ONION, DICED

1 C CELERY, DICED

1/4 C FLOUR

3 C CLAM JUICE, WARMED

1 C HALF AND HALF, WARMED

3 C OF CANNED CLAMS, CHOPPED

2 BAY LEAVES

3 C RED POTATOES, DICED

SALT AND PEPPER, TO TASTE

DIRECTIONS

IN A LARGE STOCKPOT, MELT THE BUTTER OVER MEDIUM HEAT. ADD BACON AND FRY UNTIL CRISPY. REMOVE BACON AND LET COOL.

ADD ONION AND CELERY TO STOCK POT AND COOK FOR 8 MINUTES.

SPRINKLE THE FLOUR OVER THE VEGETABLES AND STIR FOR ABOUT ONE MINUTE. GRADUALLY ADD THE CLAM JUICE AND HALF AND HALF WHILE STIRRING TO BLEND ALL INGREDIENTS.

ADD CLAMS, BAY LEAVES, AND RED POTATOES TO THE CHOWDER. SIMMER CHOWDER FOR 20-30 MINUTES UNTIL POTATOES ARE FULLY COOKED. TOP EACH BOWL OF CHOWDER WITH BACON AND SERVE.

OPTIONAL GARNISHES: WHOLE CLAMS, MUSHROOMS, AND BELL PEPPER.

> "May the God of hope fill you with all joy and peace as you trust in Him, so that you may overflow with hope by the power of the Holy Spirit." - Romans 15:13

BEING IDENTIFIED WITH JESUS MEANS TO SHARE HIS VALUES AND HIS PERSPECTIVE. AS WE ACCEPT HIS AUTHORITY OF SCRIPTURE AND ALL THAT IS WRITTEN WE ARE TO HAVE HIS ATTITUDE OF LOVE TOWARDS OTHERS. OUR GOD WHO GIVES ENDURANCE AND ENCOURAGEMENT ALSO GIVES US A SPIRIT OF UNITY (VERSE 5) WHICH ALLOWS US TO LOVE OTHERS AND ACCEPT THEM AS CHRIST ACCEPTED US (VERSE 7). IN JESUS WE CAN BE WHO GOD TRULY WANTS US TO BE... A UNIFIED PEOPLE BOUND IN LOVE. ROMANS 15:13 SAYS "MAY THE GOD OF HOPE FILL YOU WITH JOY AND PEACE AS YOU TRUST IN HIM SO THAT YOU MAY OVERFLOW WITH HOPE BY THE POWER OF THE HOLY SPIRIT". GOD WHO LOVES US WANTS TO FILL US SO THAT WE MAY OVERFLOW WITH HOPE, JOY, UNITY AND LOVE.

notes...

_____

_____

_____

_____

_____

_____

_____

_____

day
06

GINGERBREAD MUFFINS

INGREDIENTS

1/2 C BUTTER, ROOM TEMPERATURE

1/2 C BROWN SUGAR

1 EGG, ROOM TEMPERATURE

3/4 C MOLASSES

3/4 C BUTTERMILK

3/4 C GREEK YOGURT

3 C ALL PURPOSE FLOUR

1 TSP BAKING SODA

1/2 TSP SALT

3 TSP PUMPKIN SPICE

DIRECTIONS

HEAT OVEN TO 375 DEGREES.

IN MIXER, COMBINE: BUTTER AND BROWN SUGAR AND MIX FOR 5 MINUTES. ADD EGG AND MIX FOR 2 MINUTES. ADD MOLASSES, BUTTERMILK AND YOGURT AND MIX ANOTHER 2 MINUTES.

ADD DRY INGREDIENTS TO THE MIX AND SLOWLY MIX UNTIL THE DOUGH IS MIXED COMPLETELY.

SCOOP DOUGH INTO GREASED MUFFIN TIN. PLACE IN OVEN AND BAKE FOR 25 MINUTES.

OPTIONAL GARNISH: TURBINADO SUGAR

> "But God demonstrates His own love for us in this: While we were still sinners, Christ died for us." - Romans 5:8

"WHILE WE WERE STILL SINNERS". WHILE WE WERE STILL REBELLING, WHILE WE WERE STILL THINKING OUR WAY WOULD BE THE BEST, WHILE WE WERE DOING EVERYTHING WE COULD TO NOT ACKNOWLEDGE GOD. THIS IS WHEN HE LOVED US. THIS IS WHEN HE SENT JESUS TO DIE FOR OUR SINS AND OFFERED US A LIFE OF TRUE FREEDOM. GOD DOESN'T LOVE US BECAUSE WE ARE GOOD ENOUGH, HE LOVES US PERIOD. WHENEVER WE FEEL UNCERTAIN ABOUT GOD'S LOVE, LET US REMEMBER THAT HE LOVED US BEFORE WE EVER THOUGHT OF TURNING TO HIM AND REMEMBER ROMANS 5:8 "BUT GOD DEMONSTRATES HIS OWN LOVE FOR US IN THIS: WHILE WE WERE STILL SINNERS, CHRIST DIED FOR US."

notes...

day 07

ALMOND SALSA

INGREDIENTS

1 RED BELL PEPPER, SEEDED AND HALVED

2 JALAPENOS, HALVED

1 ONION, HALVED

2 ROMA TOMATOES, HALVED

2 TBSP OLIVE OIL

1 C ALMONDS, SLICED

1 C WATER

3 TBSP RICE VINEGAR

1 TSP SALT

1 LIME, JUICED

DIRECTIONS

HEAT OVEN TO 350 DEGREES.

ON A SHEET PAN PLACE BELL PEPPER, JALAPENOS, ONION, TOMATOES, AND ALMONDS. POUR OLIVE OIL OVER THE INGREDIENTS. ROAST FOR 20 MINUTES AND LET IT COOL.

TRANSFER MIXTURE TO THE BLENDER AND PUREE UNTIL SMOOTH. ADD THE WATER, VINEGAR, SALT AND LIME AND BLEND.

REFRIGERATE WHEN FINISHED.

SERVE WITH: TACOS, SWEET POTATOES, QUESADILLAS, BURRITOS, OR TAQUITOS.

"... Now is your time of grief, but I will see you again and you will rejoice, and no one will take away your joy." - John 16:22

DURING THE LAST SUPPER, JESUS USED THIS TIME TO TEACH, COMFORT, ENCOURAGE AND EXHORT HIS DISCIPLES AND ALL WHO WOULD CHOOSE TO FOLLOW HIM IN FUTURE GENERATIONS. JESUS SAYS IN JOHN 16:22 "NOW IS YOUR TIME OF GRIEF BUT I WILL SEE YOU AGAIN AND YOU WILL REJOICE AND NO ONE WILL TAKE AWAY YOUR JOY." JESUS WAS REFERRING TO HIS DEATH WHICH WAS JUST A FEW HOURS AWAY AND THEN HIS RESURRECTION THREE DAYS LATER. JESUS CARES SO MUCH FOR EACH ONE OF HIS DEAR CHILDREN. HE KNEW THE ABJECT SORROW THEY WOULD FEEL AT HIS EXECUTION, BUT HE WAS GIVING THEM HOPE THAT THE TIME OF JOY WOULD COME AND THIS JOY WOULD NEVER BE SNATCHED AWAY FROM THEM OR, SUBSEQUENTLY, FROM US.

notes...

_____
_____
_____
_____
_____
_____
_____
_____
_____
_____

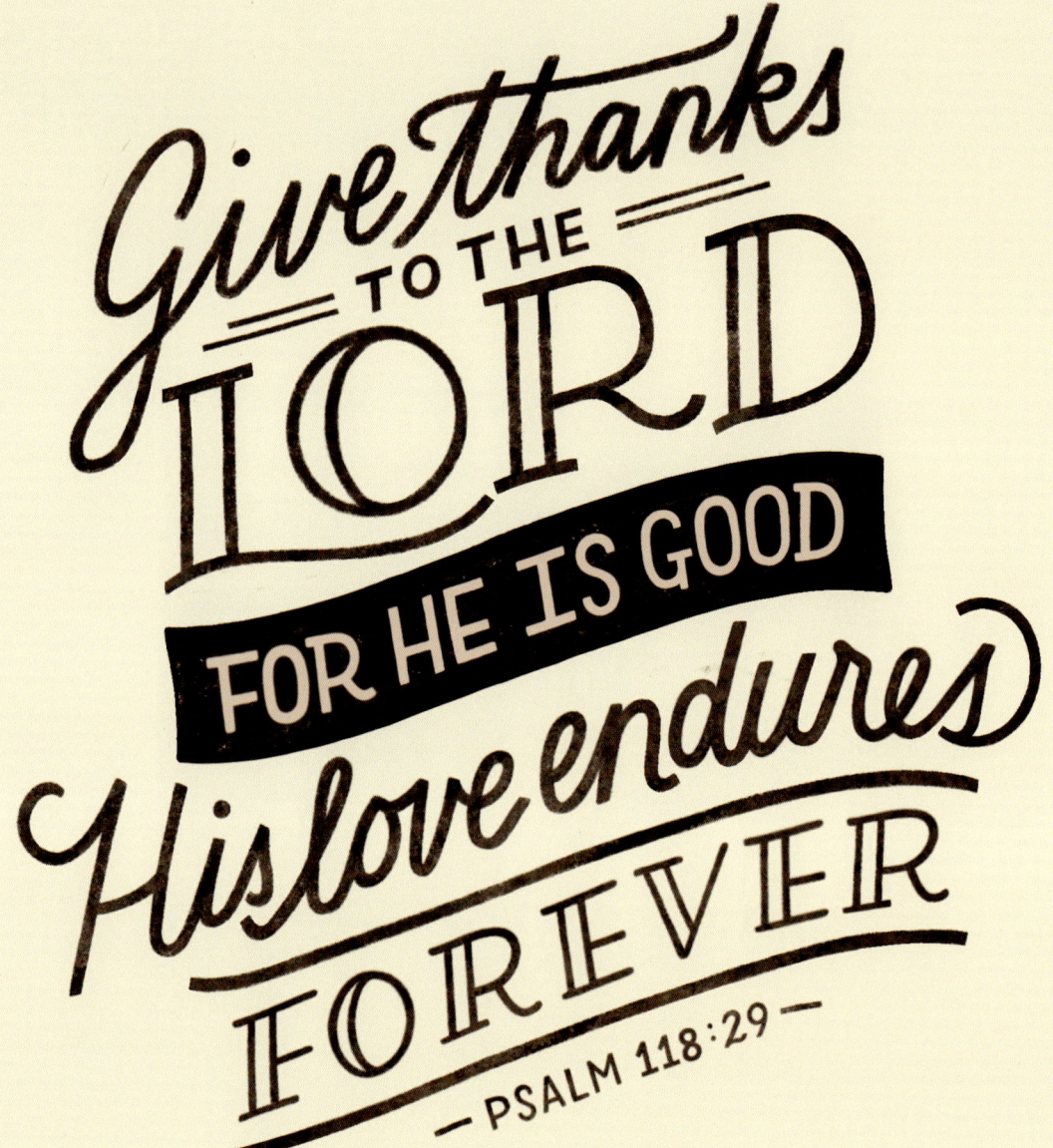

day 08

CHURROS

INGREDIENTS

1 C WATER
1/4 C BUTTER
1/4 TSP SALT
1 C FLOUR
3 EGGS
8 C OIL FOR FRYING
1/2 C SUGAR
1 TSP CINNAMON

DIRECTIONS

COMBINE WATER, BUTTER, AND SALT IN A MEDIUM SAUCE PAN, AND HEAT TO BOILING.

STIR IN FLOUR AND MIX VIGOROUSLY UNTIL IT FORMS A BALL, ABOUT ONE MINUTE.

REMOVE FROM HEAT. IMMEDIATELY, USING A MIXER, ADD EGGS, ONE AT A TIME UNTIL THE DOUGH COMES TOGETHER, AND IS SMOOTH.

HEAT OIL TO 350 DEGREES FOR FRYING THE CHURRO DOUGH ONCE THEY ARE FORMED.

USE A ZIPPED BAG OR A PIPING BAG, AND CUT OFF THE TIP, 1 INCH LONG. MAKE EACH DOUGH STRIP 4 INCHES LONG.

FRY THE CHURRO STRIPS 1 1/2 MINUTES PER SIDE. FLIP EACH ONE USING TONGS.

NEXT TAKE OUT A SHEET PAN AND LINE IT WITH A PAPER TOWEL. PLACE EACH FINISHED PIECE OF DOUGH ONTO PAPER TOWEL LINED TRAY.

NEXT COMBINE SUGAR AND CINNAMON. DIP FRIED CHURRO INTO CINNAMON SUGAR MIXTURE AND SERVE!

"But if we hope for what we do not yet have, we wait for it patiently." - Romans 8:25

HOPE IS DEFINED "TO DESIRE WITH EXPECTATION OR FULFILLMENT, TO WANT SOMETHING TO HAPPEN OR BE TRUE". WE ALL LIVE WITH HOPE, IF WE DIDN'T THEN LIFE WOULD JUST BECOME ONE LONG DRUDGERY. WE HAVE HOPE FOR OUR DAY AND OUR PLANS AND FOR WHAT OUR FUTURE MAY HOLD. ROMANS 8:24-25 TELLS US OF THE HOPE WE HAVE IN JESUS. "FOR IN THIS HOPE WE ARE SAVED." WE CAN BE CONFIDENT IN OUR SALVATION IF WE HAVE TAKEN THE STEP OF FAITH TO RECEIVE JESUS AS LORD AND SAVIOR OF OUR LIFE. OUR HEAVENLY FATHER NEVER MAKES PROMISES HE WON'T KEEP. AS WE WAIT FOR GOD'S WILL TO UNFOLD, WE CAN PLACE OUR CONFIDENCE IN GOD'S GOODNESS AND WISDOM. THIS IS A HOPE THAT WILL NEVER DISAPPOINT.

notes...

day 09

BEER MARINATED TRI TIP

INGREDIENTS

1 C BEER, YOUR PREFERENCE

2 TBSP OLIVE OIL

1 TBSP GARLIC POWDER

2 TSP DRIED OREGANO

1 TSP SALT

1/4 TSP PEPPER

1 ONION, CHOPPED

3 GARLIC CLOVES

5 LB TRI TIP ROAST

DIRECTIONS

IN A LARGE BOWL, MIX TOGETHER BEER, OLIVE OIL, GARLIC POWDER, OREGANO, SALT, PEPPER, ONION AND GARLIC. ADD TRI TIP AND EVENLY COAT IT IN THE MARINADE. COVER AND LET IT SIT FOR 30 MINUTES.

HEAT YOUR GRILL TO MEDIUM HEAT. LIGHTLY OIL THE GRILL RACK. REMOVE TRI TIP FROM MARINADE AND PLACE ON GRILL. COVER AND GRILL 10 MINUTES. MOVE TRI TIP TO COOLER PART OF GRILL, AND GRILL FOR 10-18 MORE MINUTES, DEPENDING ON YOUR PERSONAL PREFERENCE.

TAKE OFF GRILL, AND PLACE ON CUTTING BOARD AND LET IT REST FOR 10 MINUTES. SLICE AGAINST GRAIN AND SERVE.

"He got up, rebuked the wind and said to the waves, "Quiet! Be still!" Then the wind died down and it was completely calm."
- Mark 4:39

MARK 4:35-41 FINDS THE DISCIPLES WITH JESUS IN A BOAT ON THE SEA OF GALILEE. NOW MOST OF THESE MEN WERE SEASONED FISHERMEN BUT WHEN THE STORM THREATENED TO DESTROY THEM, THEY PANICKED. IN VERSE 38 THEY ACTUALLY CRY OUT, "TEACHER, DON'T YOU CARE IF WE DROWN?" JESUS THEN GOT UP, REBUKED THE WIND AND WAVES AND SAID "QUIET! BE STILL!" AND COMPLETE CALM FOLLOWED. THIS WAS A PHYSICAL STORM, BUT STORMS CAN COME IN ALL FORMS AS WE ALL KNOW. WHATEVER STORM WE FACE WE HAVE TWO CHOICES: WORRY, ASSUMING JESUS DOESN'T CARE OR RESIST FEAR AND PUT OUR TOTAL TRUST IN THE ONE WHO CAN CALM ANY STORM WE MAY FIND OURSELVES IN.

notes...

_____

_____

_____

_____

_____

_____

_____

_____

day 10

SLOW ROASTED FRENCH DIP SANDWICH

INGREDIENTS

4 LB TRI TIP ROAST

2 TBSP OLIVE OIL

1 TSP SALT

1/2 TSP PEPPER

2 C BEEF BROTH

1 TBSP SOY SAUCE

1 TBSP WORCHESTERSHIRE SAUCE

2 BAY LEAVES

6 HOAGIE ROLLS

10-12 GOUDA CHEESE SLICES, OPTIONAL

DIRECTIONS

COAT TRI TIP WITH OLIVE OIL, SALT AND PEPPER, HEAT A LARGE SKILLET TO MEDIUM HIGH. BROWN EACH SIDE OF THE TRI TIP FOR 4 MINUTES PER SIDE.

PLACE THE TRI TIP ROAST IN A SLOW COOKER/CROCKPOT. ADD TO SLOW COOKER: BROTH, SOY, WORCHESTERSHIRE, AND BAY LEAVES. COOK ON LOW FOR 8-10 HOURS.

REMOVE ROAST FROM SLOW COOKER AND SHRED. SAVE THE BROTH FOR AU JUS DIPPING SAUCE. PLACE ROAST ON HOAGIE ROLLS WITH A SLICE OF GOUDA CHEESE ON IT.

BROIL IN OVEN UNTIL CHEESE MELTS (3-4 MINUTES). SERVE FRENCH DIP SANDWICH IMMEDIATELY WITH A CUP OF AU JUS ON THE SIDE FOR DIPPING.

"And now these three remain: faith, hope and love. But the greatest of these is love."
-1 Corinthians 13:13

1 CORINTHIANS 13 IS WELL KNOWN TO MANY AS THE "LOVE" CHAPTER. MANY MARRIAGE CEREMONIES INCLUDE VERSES 4-8 WHICH DESCRIBES WHAT LOVE SHOULD AND SHOULD NOT LOOK LIKE. VERSE 13 SUMMARIZES THE CHAPTER SAYING "AND NOW THESE THREE REMAIN: FAITH, HOPE AND LOVE. BUT THE GREATEST OF THESE IS LOVE." PAUL WAS SPEAKING TO A MORALLY CORRUPT CORINTH WHERE THE WORD LOVE HELD LITTLE MEANING. TODAY, PEOPLE ARE STILL MIXING UP TRUE LOVE. LOVE IS AN ATTRIBUTE OF GOD HIMSELF, AND IT INVOLVES UNSELFISH SERVICE TO OTHERS AND TO EXHIBIT SUCH LOVE GIVES EVIDENCE THAT WE KNOW GOD. THIS TYPE OF LOVE, A LOVE PATTERNED AFTER GOD'S LOVE FOR US, WILL NEVER FAIL.

notes...

day *11*

SPANAKOPITA PIE

INGREDIENTS

4 C SPINACH, CHOPPED

1 TBSP OLIVE OIL

1 C GREEN ONIONS, THINLY SLICED

3 EGGS, BEATEN

2 1/2 C FETA, CRUMBLED

1 TBSP FRESH DILL, CHOPPED

1 TSP FRESH GARLIC, MINCED

1 C BUTTER, MELTED

1 LB PHYLLO DOUGH, DEFROSTED

DIRECTIONS

HEAT OVEN TO 375 DEGREES.

IN A LARGE BOWL, ADD THE FILLING INGREDIENTS: SPINACH, OIL, GREEN ONIONS, EGGS, FETA, DILL AND GARLIC.

BRUSH THE BOTTOM AND SIDES OF A 9X13 BAKING DISH WITH BUTTER.

UNWRAP THE PHYLLO SHEETS. WORKING QUICKLY, BRUSH THE TOP PHYLLO SHEET WITH BUTTER AND SET IT IN THE PAN. REPEAT BRUSHING BUTTER TO PHYLLO STACK AND LAYER IN THE 9X13 PAN. LAYER 10 MORE SHEETS.

SPREAD THE FILLING EVENLY OVER THE TOP OF THE 10 SHEETS OF PHYLLO. TO COVER FILLING, BUTTER A PHYLLO SHEET AND PLACE ON TOP OF FILLING. REPEAT LAYERING WITH 8 MORE PHYLLO SHEETS.

PLACE IN OVEN AND BAKE 20-25 MINUTES. ALLOW TO COOL 10 MINUTES, THEN SERVE.

"... whatever is true, whatever is noble, whatever is right, whatever is pure, whatever is lovely, whatever is admirable – if anything is excellent or praiseworthy – think about such things." - Philippians 4:8

One of the first verses I memorized when I became a Christian was Philippians 4:6-7 which begins "Do not be anxious about anything" yet my mind and my thoughts felt like a runaway train even while constantly claiming these verses. Years later, I realized that Philippians 4:8 was the key to a mind controlled by God. Thinking on things that are true, noble, right, pure, lovely, admirable, excellent or praiseworthy will focus our mind and allow anxieties to be replaced with the peace God offers. His peace transcends all understanding (verse 7). What we put in our mind determines what comes out in our words and actions. We must ask God to help us focus our mind on that which is good and pure.

notes...

day 12

FRENCH ONION SOUP

INGREDIENTS

8 C ONION, THINLY SLICED

1/2 C BUTTER

1/2 C CABERNET WINE

12 C BEEF BROTH

2 BAY LEAVES

SALT AND PEPPER, TO TASTE

1 BAGUETTE, SLICED

3 C GRUYERE CHEESE

1 C GRUYERE CHEESE, FOR TOPPING

DIRECTIONS

IN LARGE DUTCH OVEN, OVER MEDIUM HEAT, COOK ONIONS AND BUTTER. CARAMELIZE THE ONIONS BY COOKING THEM FOR 25 MINUTES.

ADD THE CABERNET TO DEGLAZE THE DUTCH OVEN AND REDUCE HEAT TO LOW FOR 5 MINUTES UNTIL THICKENED.

ADD BROTH AND BAY LEAVES AND SIMMER FOR 35 MINUTES.

HEAT OVEN TO 400 DEGREES.

PLACE BAGUETTE SLICES ON A SHEET PAN AND COVER EACH WITH CHEESE. BAKE FOR 15 MINUTES UNTIL CHEESE IS MELTED.

PLACE SOUP IN BOWLS. TOP EACH BOWL OF SOUP WITH 2 CHEESE BAGUETTE SLICES AND TOP EACH SLICE WITH MORE CHEESE (ABOUT 2 TBSP OF CHEESE). BROIL FOR FOUR MINUTES, UNTIL CHEESE IS MELTED.

"Humble yourselves, therefore, under God's mighty hand, that He may lift you up in due time."
- 1 Peter 5:8

THE WORD HUMBLE IS DEFINED AS NOT PROUD OR HAUGHTY, NOT ARROGANT OR ASSERTIVE. WE ARE ENCOURAGED IN 1 PETER 5:8 TO HUMBLE OURSELVES UNDER GOD'S MIGHTY HAND THAT HE MAY LIFT US UP IN DUE TIME. THIS KIND OF HUMILITY ISN'T LAYING DOWN AND GIVING UP BUT RATHER HUMBLY OBEYING GOD REGARDLESS OF OUR PRESENT CIRCUMSTANCES. IT MEANS NOT WORRYING ABOUT OUR POSITION OR STATUS OR RIGHTS BUT REMEMBERING THAT GOD'S RECOGNITION COUNTS MUCH MORE THAN ANY HUMAN PRAISE. GOD IS ABLE AND WILLING TO BLESS US BUT IT WILL BE ACCORDING TO HIS TIMING AND NOT OUR OWN.

notes...

day 13

ALMOND PASTE

INGREDIENTS

2 C ALMOND FLOUR

2 C SUGAR

2 EGG WHITES

2 TSP ALMOND EXTRACT

DIRECTIONS

IN A MIXER, COMBINE ALL FOUR INGREDIENTS TO MAKE ONE BALL OF PASTE.

DIVIDE INTO 3 SEGMENTS OF ALMOND PASTE, AROUND 1 C PER SEGMENT. PLACE IN ZIPPED BAGS IN FREEZER. DEFROST BEFORE USE.

USE IN: DUTCH ALMOND TART (BOTERKOEK), BISCOTTI, MACAROONS, AND SCONES.

> "... Always be prepared to give an answer to everyone who asks you to give the reason for the hope that you have. But do this with gentleness and respect."
> - 1 Peter 3:15

Each of us has our own way we feel comfortable sharing our faith. Some of us feel it is a personal matter that should be shown in our deeds and not vocally while others love to share their faith with anyone they encounter. One thing is always going to be true no matter how we choose to share the hope and light of Jesus. We must never be boisterous or obnoxious in sharing our faith but should always be ready to give an answer, gently and respectfully, when asked about our faith or Christian perspective. 1 Peter 3:15 says to always be prepared to give an answer to anyone who wonders about the hope we have. We are also told to do so with gentleness and respect. Sharing in this manner will effectively spread the light and hope of Jesus Christ.

notes...

_____

_____

_____

_____

_____

_____

_____

day 14

DUTCH PANCAKES

INGREDIENTS

6 EGGS

2 C WHOLE MILK

1/4 C BUTTER, MELTED AND COOLED

2 C ALL PURPOSE FLOUR

1/2 C BUTTER, COLD AND SLICED INTO 1 TSP SLICES

DIRECTIONS

MAKE BATTER THE NIGHT BEFORE YOU WOULD LIKE TO USE IT. IN BLENDER COMBINE: EGGS, MILK, MELTED BUTTER AND SLOWLY ADD FLOUR. BLEND AND REFRIGERATE.

IN THE MORNING, HEAT CREPE PANS (OR FRYING PANS) AND ADD 1 TSP BUTTER TO EACH PAN. SCOOP 1/2 C BATTER (OR LESS DEPENDING ON SIZE OF PAN), SWIRL BATTER AROUND THE WHOLE PAN, BROWN AND FLIP OVER. ONCE FLIPPED, WAIT UNTIL THE OTHER SIDE IS BROWNED. CONTINUE UNTIL ALL BATTER IS USED.

SERVE WITH: MAPLE SYRUP, LYLES GOLDEN SYRUP, POWDERED SUGAR, BROWN SUGAR, CINNAMON SUGAR, FRUIT AND WHIPPED CREAM.

"... continue to live in Him, rooted and built up in Him, strengthened in the faith as you were taught, and overflowing with thankfulness."
- Colossians 2:6-7

notes...

THE VERSES ABOVE END WITH "OVERFLOWING WITH THANKFULNESS". WE ALL HAVE TIMES WHEN WE ARE TRULY THANKFUL BUT TO BE OVERFLOWING WITH THANKFULNESS SEEMS A BIT UNREALISTIC. IT IS POSSIBLE BY DOING WHAT PROCEEDS THESE VERSES. "CONTINUE TO LIVE IN HIM, ROOTED AND BUILT UP IN HIM, STRENGTHENED IN THE FAITH." JUST AS PLANTS DRAW NOURISHMENT FROM THE SOIL THROUGH THEIR ROOTS, WE TOO WILL DRAW LIFE GIVING STRENGTH FROM BEING ROOTED IN CHRIST. WHEN JESUS IS OUR STRENGTH, WE WILL BE FREE OF ALL THAT WEIGHS US DOWN AND THAT IS WHEN WE WILL BE ABLE TO LIVE A LIFE OVERFLOWING WITH THANKFULNESS.

day 15

RACK OF LAMB

INGREDIENTS

6 RIB RACK OF LAMB

2 C SOY SAUCE

1/4 C OIL

6 GARLIC CLOVES, MINCED

1/2 TBSP CRUSHED RED PEPPER

DIRECTIONS

IN A ZIPPED BAG, PLACE ALL OF THE INGREDIENTS. TURN THE BAG A FEW TIMES TO MIX AND COVER THE RACK OF LAMB. MARINATE 4-18 HOURS BEFORE GRILLING.

CLEAN AND OIL GRILL. HEAT ONE SIDE OF THE GRILL. PLACE FAT SIDE DOWN ON HOT SIDE OF GRILL, COOK FOR 5 MINUTES.

TRANSFER TO THE COOLER SIDE OF THE GRILL, CLOSE LID AND COOK FOR 15-20 MINUTES (INTERNAL TEMPERATURE OF 130 DEGREES).

REMOVE FROM HEAT, WRAP IN PARCHMENT PAPER THEN FOIL, AND REST 10 MINUTES.

BEFORE SERVING, SLICE ALONG EACH RIB AND POUR THE MEAT JUICES OVER THE RIBS FOR ADDITIONAL FLAVOR.

"They will enter Zion with singing; everlasting joy will crown their heads. Gladness and joy will overtake them, and sorrow and sighing will flee away." - Isaiah 35:10

ISAIAH 35 IS ENTITLED "JOY OF THE REDEEMED" AND IT IS A BEAUTIFUL PICTURE OF GOD'S FINAL KINGDOM WHERE HE WILL ESTABLISH JUSTICE AND DESTROY ALL EVIL. IT DEPICTS A PLACE WHERE THE DAYS WILL BE PEACEFUL, AND EVERYTHING WILL BE MADE RIGHT. VERSE 10 TELLS US "THEY WILL ENTER ZION WITH SINGING; EVERLASTING JOY WILL CROWN THEIR HEADS. GLADNESS AND JOY WILL OVERTAKE THEM, AND SORROW AND SIGHING WILL FLEE AWAY." GOD IS PREPARING A PLACE FOR US, AND HE WILL WALK WITH US IN THIS LIFE, POINTING THE WAY AS WE TRAVEL HOMEWARD. GOD NEVER STOPS AT SIMPLY POINTING THE WAY BUT IS ALWAYS BESIDE US AS WE TRAVEL.

notes...

day 16

CHICKEN STUFFED CREPES

INGREDIENTS

2 TBSP BUTTER

2 C COOKED CHICKEN, CHOPPED

1 1/2 BABY BELLO MUSHROOMS, SLICED

1/4 C BUTTER

1/4 C FLOUR

1 C CHICKEN BROTH, WARMED

1 C CREAM, WARMED

1/2 C PARMESAN, GRATED

1/4 TSP NUTMEG

10-12 CREPES (OR DUTCH PANCAKES FROM DAY 14)

DIRECTIONS

HEAT OVEN TO 350 DEGREES AND GREASE A 9X13 DISH.

HEAT 2 TBSP BUTTER IN A LARGE PAN OVER MEDIUM HEAT. ADD THE CHICKEN AND THE MUSHROOMS AND COOK FOR 5 MINUTES. REMOVE FROM HEAT.

IN A MEDIUM PAN, MELT BUTTER, ADD FLOUR, MIX AND COOK FOR ABOUT 1 MINUTE.

POUR CHICKEN BROTH AND CREAM OVER THE BUTTER/FLOUR MIXTURE AND WHISK. CONTINUE COOKING ON MEDIUM HIGH UNTIL MIXTURE THICKENS, ABOUT 1-2 MINUTES. ADD PARMESAN AND NUTMEG TO THE SAUCE. SEASON WITH SALT AND BLACK PEPPER, IF NECESSARY.

ADD THE WHITE SAUCE TO THE MUSHROOM CHICKEN MIX. STIR TO COMBINE.

LAY THE CREPE ON A PLATE AND MAKE A LINE OF CHICKEN AND MUSHROOM MIX DOWN THE MIDDLE OF THE CREPE. ROLL IT UP AND PLACE IN THE BUTTERED 9X13 DISH. CONTINUE TO DO THIS WITH ALL CREPES. BAKE FOR 15 MINUTES.

"In purity, understanding, patience and kindness; in the Holy Spirit and in sincere love"
- 2 Corinthians 6:6

THIS VERSE IN 2 CORINTHIANS FALLS RIGHT IN THE MIDDLE OF A SECTION WHERE PAUL IS TALKING TO THE CORINTHIANS ABOUT HIS HARDSHIPS. IN EVERYTHING THAT PAUL DID, HE CONSIDERED WHAT HIS ACTIONS COMMUNICATED ABOUT JESUS. IF YOU ARE A BELIEVER, YOU ARE AN AMBASSADOR FOR GOD. VERSE 6 SAYS, "IN PURITY, UNDERSTANDING, PATIENCE AND KINDNESS; IN THE HOLY SPIRIT AND IN SINCERE LOVE". IN THE COURSE OF EACH DAY, PEOPLE OBSERVE US AND WHAT A BALM TO THEIR SOUL IF THESE TRAITS ARE WHAT THEY SEE BECAUSE IT IS WHAT WE EXHIBIT NO MATTER WHAT HARDSHIP WE ARE FACING. LET US NOT ALLOW OUR UNDISCIPLINED ACTIONS TO BE SOMEONE'S EXCUSE FOR REJECTING JESUS.

notes...

day 17

CROQUE MONSIEUR

INGREDIENTS

20 - 1 1/2 INCH CUBES OF CRUSTLESS BREAD

6 TBSP BUTTER, DIVIDED IN HALF

3 TBSP FLOUR

1/2 C WHOLE MILK, WARMED

2 C CHEESE, GRATED

1/3 C HAM, FINELY DICED

SALT AND PEPPER, TO TASTE

DIRECTIONS

HEAT OVEN TO 375 DEGREES.

IN A BOWL, TOSS THE BREAD CUBES WITH 3 TBSP OF MELTED BUTTER. ARRANGE THE CUBES ON A PARCHMENT LINED SHEET PAN AND BAKE FOR 8 MINUTES.

INCREASE THE OVEN TEMPERATURE TO 425 DEGREES. IN A SAUCE PAN MELT 3 TBSP OF BUTTER AND WHISK IN 3 TBSP FLOUR OVER MEDIUM HEAT FOR 1 MINUTE. WHISK IN THE MILK UNTIL THICKENED. REMOVE FROM HEAT AND ADD CHEESE AND HAM. SEASON WITH SALT AND PEPPER.

SPOON THE CHEESE FILLING ONTO THE CUBED BREAD. BAKE FOR 10 MINUTES UNTIL THE CHEESE IS MELTED AND SERVE.

GARNISH WITH AN EGG AND IT BECOMES CROQUE MADAME.

> "My command is this: Love each other as I have loved you."
> - John 15:12

AS I TURNED TO JOHN 15:12 AND LOOKED AT THE FOOTNOTES FOR 15:12-13 I HAD WRITTEN ONE WORD "SHOCKEY" (MY MOTHER-IN-LAW). IN THESE VERSES JESUS SAYS "MY COMMAND IS THIS: LOVE EACH OTHER AS I HAVE LOVED YOU. GREATER LOVE HAS NO ONE THAN THIS, THAT HE LAY DOWN HIS LIFE FOR HIS FRIENDS". JESUS IS COMMANDING US TO LOVE WITH A LOVE THAT IS SACRIFICIAL. DURING THIS TIME OF MY LIFE, JESUS WAS TEACHING ME WHAT IT LOOKS LIKE TO LOVE SACRIFICIALLY. IT DIDN'T REQUIRE ME LAYING DOWN MY LIFE FOR MY MOTHER-IN-LAW BUT IT DID INVOLVE LISTENING, HELPING, ENCOURAGING AND GIVING. JESUS IS COMMANDING US TO GIVE ALL THE LOVE WE CAN AND THEN TRY AND GIVE EVEN MORE.

notes...

day *18*

TEPPANYAKI FRIED RICE

INGREDIENTS

2 C LONG GRAIN RICE, UNCOOKED

4 C WATER

2 C FROZEN PEAS, THAWED

1/4 C CARROTS, GRATED

1 C ONION, DICED

2 TBSP BUTTER

4 EGGS, BEATEN

1/4 C BUTTER

1/4 C SOY SAUCE

2 C GREEN ONION, SLICED THINLY

DIRECTIONS

RINSE RICE WITH WATER 3 TIMES IN A STRAINER AND ADD TO PAN. ADD 4 C WATER AND BRING TO A BOIL. COVER AND SIMMER FOR 20 MINUTES. WHEN FINISHED COOKING, PLACE RICE IN A LARGE BOWL.

ADD THE PEAS, CARROTS AND ONIONS TO THE RICE BOWL AND TOSS TOGETHER.

HEAT UP 2 TBSP BUTTER IN A LARGE FRYING PAN OVER MEDIUM HEAT. ADD EGGS TO PAN AND SCRAMBLE UNTIL COOKED (ABOUT 2-3 MINUTES). TAKE OUT EGGS AND SET ASIDE. ADD 1/4 C BUTTER, COOKED RICE AND SCRAMBLED EGG BOWL TO THE LARGE FRYING PAN AND HEAT TO MEDIUM HIGH HEAT TO FRY.

ADD THE SOY SAUCE AND GREEN ONIONS AND STIR THE FRIED RICE FOR 10 MINUTES, THEN SERVE.

> "And we pray this in order that you may live a life worthy of the Lord and may please Him in every way: bearing fruit in every good work, growing in the knowledge of God" - Colossians 1:10

COLOSSIANS 1:9-14 RECORDS A PRAYER PATTERN OF PAUL'S. IN THIS SECTION, HE IS SPECIFICALLY PRAYING FOR THE COLOSSIANS, BUT HIS PRAYER CAN BE USED AS A PATTERN FOR US AS WELL. PAUL HAD NEVER MET THE COLOSSIANS BUT THAT DIDN'T HINDER HIM FROM PRAYING FOR THEM. WHEN WE PRAY FOR THOSE KNOWN OR UNKNOWN TO US WE CAN ASK THAT THEY (1) UNDERSTAND GOD'S WILL, (2) GAIN SPIRITUAL WISDOM, (3) PLEASE AND HONOR GOD, (4) BEAR GOOD FRUIT, (5) GROW IN THE KNOWLEDGE OF GOD, (6) BE FILLED WITH GOD'S STRENGTH, (7) HAVE ENDURANCE AND PATIENCE AND FINALLY (8) BE FILLED WITH CHRIST'S JOY AND GIVE THANKS ALWAYS.

notes...

_____

_____

_____

_____

_____

_____

_____

_____

day 19

DOUBLE SPLIT PEA SOUP

INGREDIENTS

4 C DRIED PEAS, RINSED

12 C WATER

1 ONION, DICED

1 1/2 GOLD POTATOES, DICED

2 GARLIC CLOVES, DICED

1 C CELERY

2 BAY LEAVES

3 TSP SALT

2 TSP PEPPER

1 C FROZEN PEAS

DIRECTIONS

IN A LARGE STOCK POT, ADD DRIED PEAS AND WATER. BRING TO A BOIL, THEN SIMMER FOR 30 MINUTES. SKIM FOAM OFF THE TOP.

ADD ONION, POTATO, GARLIC, CELERY, BAY LEAVES, SALT AND PEPPER. SIMMER 2 HOURS.

THE LAST 15 MINUTES, ADD FROZEN PEAS FOR COLOR. IF YOU LIKE CHUNKY LEAVE AS IS, IF YOU LIKE SMOOTH, JUST BLEND ALL OF IT IN BLENDER.

OPTIONAL GARNISHES: CREAM, JALAPENO, OR PARSLEY.

"For this very reason, make every effort to add to your faith goodness; and to goodness, knowledge;"- 2 Peter 1:5

OUR FAITH IS MORE THAN AN ISOLATED EVENT OR A MOMENTARY ACTION. IT MUST BE ACTIVE AND VIBRANT IF WE ARE TO POSSESS THE CHARACTER TRAITS THAT ALLOW US TO RESEMBLE WHAT JESUS DESIRES OF US. 2 PETER 1:5 SAYS, "MAKE EVERY EFFORT TO ADD TO OUR FAITH GOODNESS; AND TO GOODNESS KNOWLEDGE". KNOWING GOD BETTER, DOING HIS WILL AND LOVING OTHERS ARE ALL QUALITIES THAT DON'T HAPPEN AUTOMATICALLY. THEY TAKE HARD WORK AND MUST BE A CONTINUAL PROCESS IN A CHRISTIAN'S LIFE. AS WE KNOW GOD BETTER, HE WILL ENABLE US TO LEARN AND GROW AND LOVE OTHERS AS HE DOES. IT IS A LIFELONG PROCESS BUT IF WE KEEP CHIPPING AWAY AT OUR OLD SELF, WE WILL SEE CHRIST-LIKE QUALITIES EMERGING IN OUR LIFE.

notes...

day 20

LITTLE GEM DUTCH SALAD

INGREDIENTS FOR DRESSING

1/3 C RICE VINEGAR

1/3 C SUGAR

2 TBSP WORCHESTERSHIRE SAUCE

1 C MAYONNAISE

SALT AND PEPPER, TO TASTE

INGREDIENTS FOR SALAD

10 C LITTLE GEM OR BUTTER LETTUCE, RINSED AND CHOPPED

4 EGGS, HARD BOILED AND SLICED

4 BACON SLICES, COOKED AND CRUMBLED

1/2 C RED ONION, SLICED

1/4 C GREEN ONION, SLICED

DIRECTIONS

SHAKE ALL THE DRESSING INGREDIENTS TOGETHER AND REFRIGERATE UNTIL USE.

IN A LARGE SALAD BOWL, ADD LETTUCE AND TOP WITH EGGS, BACON, RED ONION, AND GREEN ONION.

TOSS WITH DRESSING AND SERVE IMMEDIATELY.

> "and to knowledge, self-control; and to self-control, perseverance; and to perseverance, godliness"
> - 2 Peter 1:6

KNOWLEDGE, SELF-CONTROL, PERSEVERANCE AND GODLINESS. WHAT A DAUNTING LIST OF ATTRIBUTES PETER LISTS HERE THAT WE ARE TO BE ADDING TO OUR FAITH. AT VARIOUS TIMES IN OUR LIVES, WE MIGHT THINK WE ARE DOING WELL AT SOME OF THEM, MAYBE EVEN MOST, BUT THEN WE HAVE AN EPIC FAIL AND WE FEEL DEVASTATED. IF WE LOOK AT THIS LIST AS A CHECKLIST THAT DEFINES HOW GOOD WE ARE, WE WILL ALWAYS FALL SHORT. INSTEAD, IF WE LOOK AT IT AS AN OUTPOURING OF THE HOLY SPIRIT LIVING IN US, WE WILL BE EMPOWERED TO LIVE A LIFE MARKED BY AN INTIMATE RELATIONSHIP WITH A HOLY GOD. IT IS IN RELATIONSHIP, NOT A CHECKLIST, THAT WE WILL FIND FREEDOM AND HOPE.

notes...

_____

_____

_____

_____

_____

_____

_____

_____

day 21

SLOW COOKED STEEL CUT OATS

INGREDIENTS

1 C STEEL CUT OATS

3 C WATER

1 TBSP BUTTER, OPTIONAL

PINCH OF SALT

1/4 C CREAM, OPTIONAL

DIRECTIONS

IN A SMALL SLOW COOKER, ADD STEEL CUT OATS, WATER, BUTTER, SALT, AND CREAM. TURN THE DIAL TO WARM, NOT COOK, AND LET THE OATS SLOWLY WARM OVERNIGHT. IT WILL BE READY TO SERVE IN THE MORNING.

OPTIONAL ADDITIONS AFTER COOKING:
PEANUT BUTTER, BANANA, MAPLE SYRUP, BROWN SUGAR, HONEY, ALMONDS, COCONUT, FLAX SEED, JAM, AND BERRIES.

> "and to godliness, brotherly kindness; and to brotherly kindness, love." - 2 Peter 1:7

THE HOPE FOR THIS SEASON OF NOURISH DEVOTIONALS WAS TO FOCUS ON THE FRUITS OF THE SPIRIT. MY CONCORDANCE LED ME TO 2 PETER 1:5-7 WHICH LISTS MANY QUALITIES AND BEHAVIORS THAT JESUS DESIRES FOR US. UPON RECEIVING JESUS AS LORD AND SAVIOR, WE HAVE TAKEN A STEP OF FAITH AND IT IS IN OUR FAITH JOURNEY THAT WE WILL SEE GODLINESS, BROTHERLY KINDNESS AND LOVE DEVELOP IN OUR LIVES. THE POWER TO GROW DOESN'T COME FROM WITHIN US BUT FROM GOD. IT IS THE HOLY SPIRIT, GOD'S OWN SPIRIT, INDWELLING IN US THAT EMPOWERS US WITH HIS OWN MORAL GOODNESS. GOD WANTS TO PRODUCE HIS CHARACTER IN US AND AS WE YIELD TO HIM AND LEARN TO WALK IN STEP WITH HIM, WE WILL BECOME MORE LIKE HIM.

notes...

day 22

APPLE PECAN CROISSANT BREAD PUDDING

INGREDIENTS

3 EGGS

8 EGG YOLKS

5 C HALF AND HALF

1 1/2 C BROWN SUGAR

1 1/2 TSP VANILLA

6 CROISSANTS, CUT INTO 2 INCH CUBES

2 GRANNY SMITH APPLES, DICED

1 C PECANS, CHOPPED

1 TSP CINNAMON

DIRECTIONS

HEAT OVEN TO 350 DEGREES. GREASE 10X15X2 1/2 BAKING DISH.

WHISK TOGETHER: EGGS, EGG YOLKS, HALF AND HALF, BROWN SUGAR, AND VANILLA.

PLACE CROISSANTS IN THE PREPARED BAKING DISH. ADD THE APPLES, PECANS AND CINNAMON TO THE EGG MIXTURE AND POUR OVER CROISSANTS.

PLACE THE CROISSANT DISH IN A LARGER DISH OR SHEET TRAY AND FILL THE LARGER DISH WITH 1 INCH OF WATER. THIS WILL ENSURE THE PUDDING WILL BAKE EVENLY. COVER THE LARGER PAN WITH FOIL FORMING A TENT. CUT 5 SMALL HOLES IN FOIL TO ALLOW STEAM TO ESCAPE.

BAKE FOR 45 MINUTES COVERED, THEN 45 MINUTES UNCOVERED. REMOVE FROM OVEN AND SERVE WARM.

"Let the heavens rejoice, let the earth be glad; let the sea resound, and all that is in it; let the fields be jubilant and everything in them. Then all the trees of the forest will sing for joy." - Psalm 96:11-12

PRAISE FOR OUR GOD OVERFLOWS FROM HIS CREATION AND THERE SHOULD BE A NATURAL OUTPOURING OF PRAISE FROM OUR LIPS AS WELL. CAN YOU PICTURE ALL OF CREATION WORSHIPPING AND PRAISING GOD? "LET THE EARTH BE GLAD... THE SEA RESOUND... THE FIELDS BE JUBILANT... THEN ALL THE TREES OF THE FOREST WILL SING FOR JOY." AS ONE, ALL OF CREATION COMES TOGETHER IN A SPIRITUAL SYMPHONY OF PRAISE TO THEIR CREATOR. WE CAN SING TO THE LORD A NEW SONG (VERSE 1) AND DECLARE HIS GLORY AMONG THE NATIONS (VERSE 3). MAY OUR SYMPHONY OF PRAISE TO OUR CREATOR REACH THE HEAVENS!

notes...

day 23

FAJITA ROLL UPS

INGREDIENTS

1 1/2 LBS SKIRT STEAK

1 TSP SALT

1 TSP BLACK PEPPER

1 C SALSA

1/2 C OLIVE OIL

1 TSP RED CHILI FLAKES

1/2 RED ONION, CUT INTO STRIPS

1 ORANGE BELL PEPPER, CUT INTO STRIPS

1/2 C JALAPENO CHEDDAR CHEESE, CUT INTO STRIPS

8 CORN TORTILLAS

DIRECTIONS

LAY OUT THE SKIRT STEAK. CUT INTO STRIPS, APPROXIMATELY 2X7 INCHES.

SALT AND PEPPER BOTH SIDES OF THE MEAT STRIPS.

COMBINE SALSA, OLIVE OIL AND RED CHILI FLAKES. POUR INTO A ZIPPED BAG. PLACE THE SKIRT STEAK INTO THE BAG AND MARINATE IN THE REFRIGERATOR FOR 1-4 HOURS.

HEAT OVEN TO 350 DEGREES.

MEANWHILE, CUT THE ONION, PEPPER AND CHEESE INTO STRIPS. TAKE SKIRT STEAK OUT OF MARINADE, PLACE VEGETABLES AND CHEESE IN MIDDLE OF STEAK STRIPS. ROLL UP EACH STEAK AND SECURE WITH SKEWER AND TRANSFER TO SHEET PAN. ROAST IN OVEN FOR 20 MINUTES. HEAT EACH CORN TORTILLA AND SERVE WITH ROLL UPS.

OPTIONAL GARNISHES: CILANTRO AND GREEN ONION.

"He will cover you with His feathers, and under His wings you will find refuge; His faithfulness will be your shield and rampart."
- Psalm 91:4

PSALM 91 IS A BEAUTIFUL REMINDER OF HOW GOD CARES FOR US. THE PSALMIST LISTS MANY DANGERS THAT COME AGAINST US THAT WE'RE NOT PROMISED IMMUNITY. YET WE ARE TOLD THAT NO MATTER WHAT ASSAILS US WE HAVE THE SECURITY AND STABILITY OFFERED TO US BY A LOVING HEAVENLY FATHER WHO CARES FOR US AS A MOTHER CARES FOR HER YOUNG. PSALM 91:4 TELLS US "HE WILL COVER YOU WITH HIS FEATHERS AND UNDER HIS WINGS YOU WILL FINE REFUGE; HIS FAITHFULNESS WILL BE YOUR SHIELD AND RAMPART." LIKE A MOTHER BIRD OFFERS PROTECTIVE COVER UNDER HER WINGS FOR HER BABIES, GOD WILL COVER HIS PEOPLE WITH HIS VERY FAITHFULNESS. LORD HELP US TO REMEMBER THAT YOU COMPASSIONATELY CARE FOR US AND THAT YOU WILL COMFORT US NO MATTER WHAT WE ARE FACING.

notes...

_____

_____

_____

_____

_____

_____

_____

_____

day 24

CRISPY PRESSED POTATOES

INGREDIENTS

1/2 C SEA SALT

10 YUKON GOLD POTATOES

1/4 C BUTTER, MELTED

1 TBSP SALT

1 TBSP PEPPER

1 TBSP CHIVES, CHOPPED

DIRECTIONS

HEAT OVEN TO 400 DEGREES. BRING LARGE POT OF WATER TO BOIL. ADD SEA SALT AND POTATOES, AND COOK FOR 20 MINUTES. DRAIN POTATOES IN A COLANDER AND LET DRY FOR 10 MINUTES.

PLACE THE POTATOES ON A SHEET PAN, PRESS EACH POTATO WITH THE BOTTOM OF A FLAT BOTTOMED GLASS INTO AN EVEN THICKNESS.

BRUSH BUTTER ON THE TOP OF EACH POTATO. SPRINKLE WITH SALT AND PEPPER. PLACE SHEET PAN INTO THE OVEN. ROAST THE POTATOES FOR 25 MINUTES UNTIL CRISPY. GARNISH WITH CHIVES AND SERVE.

"Righteousness will be His belt and faithfulness the sash around his waist." - Isaiah 11:5

THE PURPOSE OF THE BOOK OF ISAIAH IS TO CALL THE NATION OF JUDAH BACK TO GOD AND TO TELL OF GOD'S SALVATION THROUGH THE MESSIAH. WHILE ISAIAH IS SPEAKING TO JERUSALEM, THERE ARE ALARMING PARALLELS TO OUR OWN COUNTRY. ISAIAH 11:1-5 TELLS ABOUT THE BRANCH OF JESSE WHICH IS THE PROMISED MESSIAH FROM THE LINE OF DAVID. THIS PROMISED MESSIAH IS OUR HOPE! VERSE 5 SAYS "RIGHTEOUSNESS WILL BE HIS BELT AND FAITHFULNESS THE SASH AROUND HIS WAIST." THE RIGHTEOUSNESS THAT GOD VALUES IS ACTIVELY TURNING TOWARD OTHERS AND OFFERING THEM THE HELP THEY NEED. A REVIVAL OF RIGHTEOUSNESS, JUSTICE AND FAITHFULNESS IS THE REVIVAL WE DESPERATELY NEED.

notes...

day 25

TIA'S TAQUITOS DE PAPA

INGREDIENTS

12 C WATER

8 C RED POTATOES, SLICED IN HALF

1/4 C SALT

1/2 C BUTTER, MELTED

1/4 C MILK

20 CORN TORTILLAS, ROOM TEMPERATURE

1/2 C OLIVE OIL

DIRECTIONS

HEAT OVEN TO 350 DEGREES.

POUR WATER IN LARGE POT AND ADD POTATOES AND 1/4 C SALT. BRING TO A BOIL THEN SIMMER 20 MINUTES. DRAIN AND COOL 10 MINUTES.

IN A LARGE BOWL ADD POTATOES, BUTTER AND MILK. MASH THE MIXTURE UNTIL NO BIG CHUNKS ARE LEFT.

PUT ALL 20 TORTILLAS IN OVEN FOR 5 MINUTES, JUST TO MAKE THEM PLIABLE (DO NOT PILE THEM ON TOP OF EACH OTHER).

SPOON 2-3 TBSP OF MASHED POTATO IN THE MIDDLE OF TORTILLA AND ROLL. PLACE ON A PARCHMENT LINED SHEET PAN. CONTINUE ROLLING THE TAQUITOS UNTIL ALL THE POTATOES ARE USED. BRUSH TOPS OF EACH TAQUITO WITH OIL AND PLACE IN OVEN. COOK AT 350 DEGREES FOR 30 MINUTES, UNTIL CRISPY AND LIGHTLY BROWNED. SERVE WITH GUACAMOLE AND SALSA.

"No temptation has seized you except what is common to man. And God is faithful; He will not let you be tempted beyond what you can bear."
- 1 Corinthians 10:13

THIS VERSE CAN GIVE US SO MUCH HOPE AND PEACE. OFTENTIMES WHEN WE ARE TEMPTED INTO WRONG ACTIONS OR BEHAVIORS, WE MAY FEEL THAT WE'RE THE ONLY ONE WHO GOES THROUGH THIS. THIS WAY OF THINKING MAY CAUSE US TO FEEL WEAK AND ALONE CAUSING US TO DRAW INWARD. 1 CORINTHIANS 10:13 TELLS A WHOLE DIFFERENT STORY. "NO TEMPTATION HAS SEIZED YOU EXCEPT WHAT IS COMMON TO MAN". ALL OF US ARE TEMPTED AND EACH OF US CAN RESIST BECAUSE GOD IS FAITHFUL. RECOGNIZING THOSE SITUATIONS THAT GIVE US TROUBLE AND RUNNING FROM THEM IS A START. THEN PRAY FOR GOD'S HELP AND SEEK FRIENDS WHO LOVE GOD AND CAN OFFER SUPPORT WHEN YOU NEED IT.

notes...

_____

_____

_____

_____

_____

_____

_____

day
26

EUROPEAN HOT CHOCOLATE

INGREDIENTS

2 C WHOLE MILK

1/2 C HEAVY CREAM

3/4 C DARK CHOCOLATE, CHIPS OR CHUNKS

1/2 TSP INSTANT ESPRESSO

1 C WHIPPED CREAM, GARNISH

DIRECTIONS

IN A SAUCE PAN, HEAT MILK AND CREAM ON MEDIUM HIGH UNTIL SLIGHTLY BOILING. TURN OFF HEAT AND ADD THE CHOCOLATE AND WHISK UNTIL ALL OF THE CHOCOLATE HAS MELTED. ADD THE ESPRESSO AND STIR.

POUR INTO MUG AND TOP WITH WHIPPED CREAM.

"Whoever can be trusted with very little can also be trusted with much ..." - Luke 16:10

THE FRUIT OF GOD'S HOLY SPIRIT OF FAITHFULNESS CAN TAKE ON MANY DIFFERENT FORMS. IN LUKE 16:10 JESUS IS TALKING ABOUT OUR FAITHFULNESS IN DEALING WITH OTHERS AND WITH OUR POSSESSIONS. "WHOEVER CAN BE TRUSTED WITH VERY LITTLE CAN ALSO BE TRUSTED WITH MUCH AND WHOEVER IS DISHONEST WITH VERY LITTLE IS DISHONEST WITH MUCH." WOVEN IN THIS VERSE IS NOT ONLY THE CONCEPT OF TRUSTWORTHINESS BUT FAITHFULNESS AND INTEGRITY AS WELL. GOD CALLS US TO BE HONEST IN THE SMALLEST DETAILS OF OUR LIVES THAT COULD EASILY BE RATIONALIZED AWAY AND IN DOING SO WE WILL NOT FAIL IN THE MORE CRUCIAL DECISIONS THAT COME OUR WAY.

notes...

day 27

BLOODY MARY SPICE BLEND

INGREDIENTS

3 TBSP CELERY SALT

1 TBSP OLD BAY SEASONING

1 TBSP ONION POWDER

1 TBSP GARLIC POWDER

1 TBSP PAPRIKA

1 TBSP BLACK PEPPER

1 TBSP BROWN SUGAR

1 TSP MUSTARD, DRY

DIRECTIONS

IN A LARGE JAR, ADD ALL OF THE INGREDIENTS AND SHAKE TO MIX SEASONING.

ADD TO DAY 28 LIQUID INGREDIENTS FOR A BLOODY MARY.

OPTIONAL USES: BLOODY MARY, SHRIMP, CHICKEN, OR HARD BOILED EGG.

"Surely God is my salvation; I will trust and not be afraid. The Lord, the Lord, is my strength and my song; He has become my salvation." - Isaiah 12:2

IN THE EARLY MORNING HOUR WHEN THE DAY IS BRAND NEW IT IS EASY TO HAVE AN ATTITUDE OF PRAISE. DEPENDING ON YOUR LOCATION YOU MAY EXPERIENCE VARIOUS TYPES OF BIRDS SINGING THEIR SONG OR A BROOK BABBLING OR THE SURF RHYTHMICALLY COMFORTING. DURING THIS TIME, IT'S ALMOST IMPOSSIBLE TO NOT FEEL PEACEFUL. ISAIAH 12 IS A SONG OF PRAISE TO THE LORD AND VERSE 2 SAYS "SURELY GOD IS MY SALVATION; I WILL TRUST AND NOT BE AFRAID. THE LORD, THE LORD IS MY STRENGTH AND MY SONG; HE HAS BECOME MY SALVATION" IT GOES ON TO TELL US TO GIVE THANKS TO THE LORD, TO SING TO THE LORD AND TO SING FOR JOY. MAY THIS ATTITUDE OF PRAISE TO OUR LORD BE WITH US THROUGHOUT THE DAY AND NOT ONLY AT ITS DAWN.

notes...

_____

_____

_____

_____

_____

_____

_____

day 28

HOMEMADE BLOODY MARY COCKTAIL

INGREDIENTS

16 OZ TOMATO JUICE

2 TBSP WORCHESTERSHIRE SAUCE

1 TSP PICKLE JUICE

1 TBSP TABASCO

2 TSP PEPPERONCINI JUICE

2 TBSP LIME JUICE

2 TBSP LEMON JUICE

1 TSP HORSERADISH, OPTIONAL

1 TSP SALT

4-6 OZ VODKA, OPTIONAL

2 TBSP BLOODY MARY SPICE BLEND (DAY 27)

DIRECTIONS

MIX ALL THE LIQUIDS TOGETHER IN A LARGE JAR, SHAKE TO MIX.

GRAB AN 8 OZ GLASS AND RUB A LEMON ACROSS THE RIM OF THE GLASS. ADD 2 TBSP OF BLOODY MARY SPICE BLEND ON A FLAT PLATE AND DIP THE RIM OF THE GLASS CUP ONTO THE SPICE MIX. ADD THE LIQUID, STIR, AND ENJOY!

OPTIONAL GARNISHES: CELERY, OLIVE, BACON, PICKLES, AND LIME WEDGES.

"Give thanks to the Lord, for He is good; His love endures forever." - Psalm 118:29

PSALM 118 IS ABOUT GOD'S UNCHANGING LOVE IN THE MIDST OF CHANGING CIRCUMSTANCES. THE THEME OF THE PSALM IS HAVING CONFIDENCE IN GOD'S ETERNAL LOVE. EACH OF US MUST PUT OUR CONFIDENCE IN SOMETHING OR SOMEONE DAILY BUT OUR OVERRIDING CONFIDENCE SHOULD BE IN GOD TO GUIDE US HERE ON EARTH AND TO OUR ETERNAL DESTINATION. THE REFRAIN "HIS LOVE ENDURES FOREVER" IS WOVEN THROUGHOUT THE PSALM AND VERSE 29 CLOSES WITH "GIVE THANKS TO THE LORD FOR HE IS GOOD; HIS LOVE ENDURES FOREVER." DO WE TRUST HIM MORE THAN ANY OTHER? GOD IS ETERNAL, UNCHANGING AND HE LOVES US. THIS GIVES US SECURITY IN OUR EVERCHANGING SITUATIONS.

notes...

LOVE
*is patient
is kind
does not envy
does not boast
is not proud*

1 CORINTHIANS 13:4

day
29

QUICHE LORRAINE

INGREDIENTS

1 FROZEN PIE CRUST, THAWED

3/4 C HEAVY CREAM

3/4 C MILK

4 EGGS

1 TSP SALT

1/2 TSP BLACK PEPPER

1 C BACON, COOKED AND DICED

1/2 C GOUDA CHEESE, GRATED

1/4 C CHIVES, MINCED

DIRECTIONS

HEAT OVEN TO 350 DEGREES. ROLL THE PIE CRUST AND TRANSFER INTO A PIE PLATE. PINCH THE EDGE OF THE CRUST. PLACE IN FREEZER FOR 10 MINUTES. THIS WILL MAKE THE CRUST FLAKY. REMOVE FROM FREEZER AND POKE THE DOUGH WITH A FORK IN 10 DIFFERENT PLACES. BAKE IN OVEN 30 MINUTES.

IN A LARGE BOWL, WHISK TOGETHER CREAM, MILK, EGGS, SALT AND PEPPER. ADD BACON AND CHEESE TO MIXTURE AND POUR OVER PIE CRUST. TOP WITH CHIVES.

SET THE QUICHE PAN ON A SHEET PAN AND BAKE AT 350 DEGREES FOR 45 MINUTES. SERVE WARM.

OPTIONAL ADDITIONS: JALAPENOS, POTATOES, OR SPINACH.

"Love is patient, love is kind. It does not envy, it does not boast, it is not proud."
- 1 Corinthians 13:4

1 CORINTHIANS 13: 4-8 MAY BE ONE OF THE MOST WELL-KNOWN PASSAGES IN THE BIBLE TO BELIEVERS AND NONBELIEVERS ALIKE. MANY MIGHT NOT REALIZE WHERE IT IS FROM, BUT THE WORDS ARE FAMILIAR. IN OUR CULTURE, LOVE AND LUST ARE OFTEN CONFUSED. THE KIND OF LOVE SPOKEN OF HERE COMES FROM A RIGHT RELATIONSHIP WITH GOD. THIS LOVE CALLS US TO PUT OTHERS FIRST AND IS UNSELFISH; WHEREAS, LUST IS UTTERLY SELFISH AND THINKS ONLY OF SELF. TO BE PATIENT AND KIND AND TO NOT ENVY, BOAST OR BE PROUD GOES AGAINST OUR NATURAL INCLINATIONS. IT IS POSSIBLE TO PRACTICE THIS LOVE IF, WITH GOD'S HELP, WE SET ASIDE OUR OWN DESIRES AND INSTINCTS. BY DOING SO, WE CAN LOVE OTHERS WITHOUT EXPECTING ANYTHING IN RETURN.

notes...

day 30

EASY OVERNIGHT FRIED CHICKEN

INGREDIENTS

10 CHICKEN THIGHS, BONE IN SKIN ON
1 TSP SALT
1 TSP PEPPER
3 C BUTTERMILK
3 C FLOUR, OR GLUTEN FREE FLOUR
1 C PANKO BREAD CRUMBS
2 TSP SALT
2 TSP ONION POWDER
1 1/2 TSP CAYENNE
8 C OIL

DIRECTIONS

PLACE CHICKEN THIGHS ON A SHEET PAN. SPRINKLE SALT AND PEPPER EVENLY OVER EACH PIECE OF CHICKEN. PLACE ALL PIECES IN A ZIPPED PLASTIC BAG AND POUR BUTTERMILK IN BAG. PLACE THE BAG ON A SHEET PAN AND REFRIGERATE OVERNIGHT.

IN A SHALLOW BOWL, WHISK TOGETHER FLOUR, PANKO, SALT, ONION POWDER, AND CAYENNE.

REMOVE EACH THIGH FROM MARINADE AND PLACE IN FLOUR MIXTURE TO COAT. PLACE ON SHEET PAN.

HEAT OIL IN LARGE FRYING PAN TO HIGH HEAT, OIL SHOULD BE 350 DEGREES.

PLACE 3 COATED CHICKEN THIGHS INTO OIL. TURN OVER CHICKEN UNTIL EACH SIDE IS NICELY BROWNED (ABOUT 4 MINUTES EACH SIDE). TRANSFER FINISHED PIECES TO A RACK ON A SHEET PAN. TURN ON OVEN TO 350 DEGREES.

PLACE CHICKEN IN OVEN AND FINISH BAKING. BAKE 10 MINUTES, AND FLIP CHICKEN OVER AND BAKE ADDITIONAL 10 MINUTES.

GARNISH AND SERVE.

OPTIONAL GARNISHES: HONEY, SALT, PEPPER, CHIVES AND HOT SAUCE.

"Taste and see that the Lord is good; blessed is the man who takes refuge in Him." - Psalm 34:8

PSALM 34:8 IS A WARM INVITATION TO ALL WHO WOULD SEEK THE LORD. IN ESSENCE IT'S ASKING US TO "TRY THIS, I PROMISE YOU WILL LIKE IT AND IT WILL BE GOOD FOR YOU". AS WE JOURNEY WITH GOD, WE DISCOVER THAT HE IS GOOD AND KIND AND AS OUR FAITH GROWS WE SEE THAT HE TRULY CARES FOR US. GOD PAYS ATTENTION TO ALL WHO CALL UPON HIM. SO, WHETHER IT'S ESCAPE FROM TROUBLE OR HELP IN TIMES OF TROUBLE, WE CAN REST ASSURED THAT GOD ALWAYS HEARS AND ACTS ON OUR BEHALF. ACCEPT HIS INVITATION TODAY TO "TASTE AND SEE THAT THE LORD IS GOOD".

notes...

_____

_____

_____

_____

_____

_____

_____

day 31

WINTER ROASTED VEGETABLE SALAD

INGREDIENTS FOR ROASTED VEGETABLES

2 C RED ONION, SLICED

2 C BUTTERNUT SQUASH, PEELED AND DICED

2 C RED POTATOES, HALVED

1 C CARROTS, PEELED AND DICED

2 TBSP OLIVE OIL

SALT AND PEPPER, TO TASTE

INGREDIENTS FOR SALAD

2 TBSP BALSAMIC VINEGAR

4 TBSP OLIVE OIL

4 C BABY GREENS

1 C FETA

SALT AND PEPPER, TO TASTE

DIRECTIONS

HEAT OVEN TO 400 DEGREES. GREASE A SHEET PAN. MIX ALL VEGETABLES TOGETHER (FIRST FOUR FROM ROASTED INGREDIENTS LIST) IN BOWL, ADD OLIVE OIL, THEN SALT AND PEPPER.

ROAST IN OVEN FOR 40 MINUTES.

MIX THE SALAD DRESSING TOGETHER: OIL, BALSAMIC, SALT AND PEPPER.

REMOVE ROASTED VEGETABLES FROM THE OVEN AND COOL FOR 10 MINUTES.

IN LARGE SALAD BOWL, LAYER THE BABY GREENS, ROASTED VEGETABLES, DRESSING AND FETA.

OPTIONAL GARNISHES: LEMON WEDGES AND ALMONDS.

"Be still and know that I am God; I will be exalted among the nations, I will be exalted in the earth." - Psalm 46:10

THE PSALMS ARE A COLLECTION OF WORKS BY VARIOUS AUTHORS. THE PURPOSE OF THEM IS TO PROVIDE POETRY FOR THE EXPRESSION OF PRAISE, WORSHIP AND CONFESSION TO GOD. PSALM 46:10 IS DEEPLY SOOTHING, "BE STILL AND KNOW THAT I AM GOD; I WILL BE EXALTED..." GOD'S FINAL VICTORY IS ASSURED AND AT THAT TIME WE WILL STAND BEFORE THE LORD REVERENTLY HONORING HIM AND HIS POWER AND MAJESTY OVER ALL! TAKING TIME EACH DAY TO BE STILL AND EXALT THE LORD WILL RESTORE OUR SOULS AND CENTER US FOR WHAT LIES AHEAD IN OUR DAY.

notes...

_____
_____
_____
_____
_____
_____
_____
_____
_____

day 32

SPICY YELLOW RICE SALAD WITH KALE AND VEGETABLES

INGREDIENTS

1 C JASMINE RICE, UNCOOKED

1 1/2 C COCONUT MILK

1/2 TSP TURMERIC

4 C KALE, CHOPPED

1/4 C OLIVE OIL

2 LIMES, JUICED

4 GARLIC CLOVES, MINCED

2 RED BELL PEPPERS, DICED

1 CUCUMBER, DICED

1 JALAPENO, DICED

SALT AND PEPPER, TO TASTE

DIRECTIONS

RINSE RICE IN A STRAINER. POUR RINSED RICE INTO COOKER AND ADD COCONUT MILK AND TURMERIC. COOK RICE. ONCE RICE IS FINISHED, LET COOL.

MASSAGE THE KALE WITH OLIVE OIL FOR 2 MINUTES. THEN ADD LIME JUICE, GARLIC, BELL PEPPERS, CUCUMBER AND JALAPENO. TOSS TOGETHER IN A LARGE SALAD BOWL. ADD COOKED RICE TO BOWL AND TOSS TOGETHER. SEASON WITH SALT AND PEPPER.

OPTIONAL GARNISHES: CILANTRO, BASIL, MINT, AND PEANUTS.

"Like a city whose walls are broken down is a man who lacks self-control." - Proverbs 25:28

NEHEMIAH WAS AN IMPORTANT JEWISH LEADER IN THE MID-5TH CENTURY BC. UPON HIS RELEASE FROM CAPTIVITY, HE LED A GROUP OF HIS PEOPLE BACK TO A RUINED JERUSALEM. ONE OF THE FIRST THINGS HE ORGANIZED WAS THE REBUILDING OF THE BROKEN-DOWN WALL AROUND THE CITY. ALTHOUGH THE WALL RESTRICTED MOVEMENT, IT WAS VITALLY IMPORTANT FOR PROTECTION AGAINST MANY DANGERS. SELF-CONTROL IS VERY MUCH LIKE A CITY WALL. IT MIGHT FEEL LIMITING, BUT IT IS NECESSARY TO PROTECT US FROM ALL KINDS OF ENEMY ATTACKS. THINK OF SELF-CONTROL AS A WALL FOR DEFENSE AND PROTECTION IN OUR LIVES.

notes...

_____

_____

_____

_____

_____

_____

_____

_____

day 33

PORTOBELLO PAPARADELLE

INGREDIENTS

4 TBSP BUTTER

1/2 C ONION, SLICED

1 TSP SALT

2 C PORTOBELLO OR BABY BELLO MUSHROOMS, DICED

8 OZ PAPARDELLE DRIED PASTA

3 TBSP SALT

1 C HEAVY CREAM

2 GARLIC CLOVES, MINCED

1/2 TSP RED CHILI FLAKES

1 TSP BALSAMIC VINEGAR

1 C PARMESAN, GRATED

DIRECTIONS

IN A LARGE SKILLET, MELT BUTTER OVER MEDIUM HEAT. ADD ONION, SALT, AND MUSHROOMS. STIR FOR 5 MINUTES.

MEANWHILE, BRING A LARGE STOCKPOT OF WATER TO BOIL AND ADD 3 TBSP OF SALT. ADD PAPARDELLE PASTA AND COOK PASTA ACCORDING TO INSTRUCTIONS ON PACKAGE. DRAIN PASTA.

ADD HEAVY CREAM, GARLIC, CHILI FLAKES, AND VINEGAR TO THE LARGE MUSHROOM SKILLET. MIX WELL, THEN ADD PASTA TO SKILLET AND COAT ALL THE PASTA. GARNISH WITH THE PARMESAN. SEASON WITH SALT AND PEPPER AS NEEDED.

"I waited patiently for the Lord; He turned to me and heard my cry." - Psalm 40:1

"I WAITED PATIENTLY FOR THE LORD..." OFTENTIMES WAITING ON THE LORD FOR DIRECTION AND ANSWERS IS EXTREMELY DIFFICULT AS HIS TIMING IS NOT THE SAME AS OURS. ALSO, HE SEES THE WHOLE COURSE OF OUR LIFE AND ALWAYS KNOWS WHAT'S BEST FOR US SO WHEN WE WANT SOMETHING "NOW" AND GET FRUSTRATED IN THE "WAIT" OUR ABILITY TO BE PATIENT MAY BECOME DIFFICULT. PSALM 40:1 SAYS "HE TURNED TO ME AND HEARD MY CRY" SO BE ASSURED GOD ALWAYS HEARS US. EVEN IF HE MAY SEEM QUIET, HE ALWAYS SEES AND HEARS HIS DEARLY BELOVED. SURPRISINGLY THE TRIAL OF WAITING OFTENTIMES RESULTS IN MANY BLESSINGS WE NEVER COULD HAVE ANTICIPATED.

notes...

day 34

ENDIVE AND BRIE SLIDERS

INGREDIENTS

1 LB BELGIUM ENDIVE

6 OZ BRIE CHEESE, DICED

1/4 C DRIED CRANBERRIES

1 C PECANS, TOASTED

1/4 C BALSAMIC GLAZE

PINCH OF RED CHILI FLAKES

PINCH OF CHIVES

DIRECTIONS

TRIM ENDIVE BY CUTTING OFF THE CORE AND PULLING OFF THE DAMAGED OUTER LEAVES.

ASSEMBLE THE SLIDERS ON A LARGE TRAY. EACH INDIVIDUAL ENDIVE LEAF WILL LAYER WITH BRIE, DRIED CRANBERRIES, PECANS, AND BALSAMIC GLAZE. GARNISH WITH CHILI FLAKES AND CHIVES.

"I am still confident of this; I will see the goodness of the Lord in the land of the living. Wait for the Lord; be strong and take heart and wait for the Lord." - Psalm 27:13-14

OUR GOD IS A GOOD GOD WHO ONLY WANTS WHAT IS BEST FOR US. DOES HE THINK IN THE SAME WAY WE DO? DOES HE FOLLOW THE SAME TIMELINE WE MIGHT HAVE IN MIND FOR OUR LIVES? NO, HE DOES NOT BUT HIS PLAN FOR US IS ALWAYS STEEPED IN GOODNESS. PSALM 27:13-14 TELLS US "I AM STILL CONFIDENT OF THIS; I WILL SEE THE GOODNESS OF THE LORD...WAIT FOR THE LORD." WAITING FOR THE LORD IS NOT EASY, BUT HE IS ALWAYS WORTH WAITING FOR. WHILE WE WAIT LET US TAKE THE TIME TO ALLOW GOD TO REFRESH, RENEW AND TEACH US.

notes...

day 35

PRIME RIB ROAST

INGREDIENTS FOR ROAST

- 6 LB BONE IN PRIME RIB ROAST
- 1/2 C BUTTER, MELTED
- 1 TBSP SALT
- 2 TSP BLACK PEPPER

INGREDIENTS FOR AU JUS

- 1/2 C MEAT DRIPPINGS
- 2 C BEEF BROTH
- 1 C RED WINE

DIRECTIONS

REMOVE PRIME RIB FROM REFRIGERATOR AND BRING TO ROOM TEMPERATURE, ABOUT 2 HOURS. HEAT OVEN TO 450 DEGREES.

PAT DRY THE PRIME RIB WITH PAPER TOWEL. POUR MELTED BUTTER OVER ENTIRE PRIME RIB, AND SALT AND PEPPER IT.

PLACE THE ROAST WITH THE FAT SIDE UP IN A ROASTING PAN. PLACE IN OVEN. COOK PRIME RIB FOR 20 MINUTES AT 450 DEGREES, THEN REDUCE OVEN TO 325 DEGREES. USING A MEAT THERMOMETER, CHECK THE INTERNAL TEMPERATURE OF THE PRIME RIB, AFTER AN HOUR AND A HALF. FOR MEDIUM RARE, THE INTERNAL TEMPERATURE SHOULD REACH 120 DEGREES.

REMOVE FROM OVEN. TAKE OUT PRIME RIB FROM PAN AND COVER IT WITH PARCHMENT PAPER THEN FOIL AND LET IT REST FOR 20 MINUTES.

MEANWHILE, USE THE PAN DRIPPINGS TO MAKE THE AU JUS IN A MEDIUM SAUCE PAN. ADD BROTH AND WINE TO SAUCE PAN ON MEDIUM HEAT, SIMMER FOR 15 MINUTES.

SLICE PRIME RIB INTO 1/2 INCH SLICES. SPOON AU JUS OVER EACH SLICE AND SERVE.

"I led them with cords of human kindness, with ties of love; I lifted the yoke from their neck and bent down to feed them." - Hosea 11:4

HOSEA WAS A PROPHET FROM ABOUT 753-715 BC AND HIS PURPOSE WAS TO ILLUSTRATE THE LOVE GOD HAS FOR HIS SINFUL PEOPLE. HOSEA WAS COMMANDED BY GOD TO MARRY A WOMAN NAMED GOMER, EVEN THOUGH HE KNEW SHE WOULD BE UNFAITHFUL AND CAUSE HOSEA MANY HEARTACHES. HOSEA DID WHAT GOD COMMANDED AND THROUGHOUT HIS MARRIAGE HE PURSUED, RESCUED AND HELPED RESTORE HIS WIFE. HOSEA 11:4 SPEAKS OF GOD'S LOVE FOR HIS PEOPLE, "I LED THEM WITH CORDS OF HUMAN KINDNESS, WITH TIES OF LOVE". HOSEA'S STORY IS AN ILLUSTRATION OF OUR RELATIONSHIP WITH GOD. LIKE GOMER, WE MAY CHASE AFTER OTHER LOVES — LOVE OF POWER, RICHES OR RECOGNITION. ARE WE FAITHFUL TO GOD OR HAVE OTHER LOVES TAKEN GOD'S PLACE? GOD IS A PURSUING GOD. NO MATTER HOW FAR WE'VE STRAYED, HE IS ALWAYS WILLING TO BRING US BACK.

notes...

_____

_____

_____

_____

_____

_____

_____

And now, these three remain: faith, hope, & love. But the greatest of these is love.

1 CORINTHIANS 13:13

day 36

SHORTBREAD SUGAR COOKIE

INGREDIENTS

1 C BUTTER, ROOM TEMPERATURE

3/4 C OIL

1/2 C SUGAR

1/2 C POWDERED SUGAR

2 TBSP GREEK PLAIN YOGURT

2 EGGS, ROOM TEMPERATURE

1 1/2 TSP BAKING SODA

1 TSP VANILLA

5 1/2 C ALL PURPOSE FLOUR

1/2 C GRANULATED SUGAR

DIRECTIONS

HEAT OVEN TO 350 DEGREES.

CREAM TOGETHER IN A MIXER: BUTTER, OIL AND SUGARS. MIX FOR 5 MINUTES.

SLOWLY ADD YOGURT. ADD EGGS, ONE AT A TIME. THEN ADD BAKING SODA, VANILLA AND FLOUR, LIGHTLY MIX.

SCOOP DOUGH INTO PING PONG SIZE BALLS. USE A DRINKING GLASS, DIP BOTTOM OF GLASS IN WATER, THEN DIP INTO GRANULATED SUGAR. PRESS EACH BALL DOWN, WITH BOTTOM OF GLASS TO 1/2 INCH THICK. PLACE DOUGH BALLS, SUGAR SIDE UP, ON PARCHMENT PAPER LINED SHEET PAN. BAKE FOR 10 MINUTES. IF YOU'D LIKE, USE FROSTING RECIPE BELOW, AND FROST COOKIES ONCE COOKIES ARE COOLED.

FROSTING RECIPE: 3/4 C BUTTER, 2 TBSP GREEK YOGURT, 1 TSP VANILLA, 6 C POWDERED SUGAR, 2 TBSP CREAM. MIX TOGETHER UNTIL CREAMY.

"A gentle answer turns away wrath, but a harsh word stirs up anger." - Proverbs 15:1

WE'VE ALL EITHER BEEN IN ARGUMENTS OR WITNESSED THEM FIRSTHAND. ANGRY WORDS FLY BETWEEN PEOPLE, APOLOGIES MAY OR MAY NOT BE GIVEN BUT THE WORDS THAT WERE SPOKEN IN ANGER ARE RARELY FORGOTTEN. PROVERBS 15:1 TELLS US "A GENTLE ANSWER TURNS AWAY WRATH, BUT A HARSH WORD STIRS UP ANGER". CAN YOU IMAGINE IF WE TRIED TO ARGUE IN NOTHING BUT A WHISPER? OR HOW ABOUT IF WE ONLY RESPONDED WITH A GENTLE ANSWER? WE MAY FIND THAT THE ARGUMENT RUNS OUT OF STEAM AND CAN BE AVOIDED. TO SEEK PEACE, WE MUST CHOOSE GENTLE WORDS.

notes...

day
37

CANDY CANE SHAKE

INGREDIENTS

3 C ICE

1/2 C CANDY CANES, CRUSHED

1/2 C SUGAR

2 C HEAVY CREAM

DIRECTIONS

IN BLENDER PLACE THE ICE, CANDY CANES, SUGAR AND HEAVY CREAM. BLEND ON HIGH SPEED UNTIL SMOOTH.

ENJOY WITH A SPOON OR A STRAW!

OPTIONAL GARNISHED: WHIPPED CREAM, CANDY CANE, CRUSHED CANDY CANE, AND CHOCOLATE SPRINKLES.

> "Rejoice greatly, Daughter Zion! Shout, Daughter Jerusalem! See, your king comes to you, righteous and victorious, lowly and riding on a donkey, on a colt, the foal of a donkey." - Zechariah 9:9

THIS PROPHECY WAS WRITTEN BY ZECHARIAH MORE THAN 500 YEARS BEFORE IT HAPPENED. JESUS' TRIUMPHAL ENTRY INTO JERUSALEM IS RECORDED IN MATTHEW 11:1-11 THUS FULFILLING THIS PROPHECY. ZECHARIAH 9:9 SAYS "... SEE, YOUR KING COMES TO YOU GENTLE AND RIDING ON A DONKEY, ON A COLT, THE FOAL OF A DONKEY." IN HIS BOOK, MATTHEW RECORDS JESUS' ACTIONS AND HOW THEY WERE A FULFILLMENT OF THE PROPHET'S WORDS GIVING YET ANOTHER INDICATION THAT JESUS WAS INDEED THE PROMISED MESSIAH. IN RIDING ON A DONKEY'S COLT, HE AFFIRMED HIS MESSIANIC ROYALTY AS WELL AS HIS HUMILITY. JUST AS THIS PROPHECY WAS FULFILLED, WE CAN BE CONFIDENT THAT THE PROPHECIES OF HIS SECOND COMING ARE JUST AS CERTAIN TO BE FULFILLED.

notes...

_____

_____

_____

_____

_____

_____

_____

_____

day 38

SHEET PAN SPECULAAS

INGREDIENTS

3 CUBES BUTTER, ROOM TEMPERATURE

1 C BROWN SUGAR

1 C SUGAR

2 EGGS

3 C FLOUR

1 TSP BAKING SODA

1/2 TSP NUTMEG

3 TSP CINNAMON

1 TSP CLOVES

DIRECTIONS

HEAT OVEN TO 350 DEGREES. PREPARE A SHEET PAN WITH PARCHMENT PAPER (OR A SILPAT).

CREAM THE BUTTER AND SUGARS TOGETHER IN A STAND MIXER, ABOUT 5 MINUTES.

ADD EGGS TO THE MIXTURE AND MIX FOR 2 MINUTES. SLOWLY ADD THE DRY INGREDIENTS: FLOUR, BAKING SODA, NUTMEG, CINNAMON AND CLOVES.

SPREAD THE DOUGH OVER THE PARCHMENT LINED PAN. BAKE FOR 20 MINUTES. ONCE COOLED, SLICE INTO PIECES AND SERVE.

"Rejoice in the Lord always, I will say it again: Rejoice! Let your gentleness be evident to all. The Lord is near."
- Philippians 4:4-5

AS PAUL WROTE THIS LETTER TO THE PHILIPPIANS HE WAS IMPRISONED AND YET HE TOLD THEM TO REJOICE. HOW COULD THIS EVEN BE POSSIBLE? PAUL IS TEACHING AN IMPORTANT LESSON THAT OUR ATTITUDE DOESN'T HAVE TO REFLECT OUR OUTWARD CIRCUMSTANCES. PAUL WAS FULL OF JOY IN SPITE OF HIS CIRCUMSTANCES BECAUSE HE KNEW THAT NO MATTER WHAT HAPPENED TO HIM, JESUS WAS WITH HIM. ULTIMATE JOY COMES FROM JESUS DWELLING WITHIN US. VERSE 5 GOES ON TO SAY THAT WE ARE TO "LET OUR GENTLENESS BE EVIDENT TO ALL". ATTRIBUTES OF GENTLENESS AND JOY WILL ALLOW US TO BE REASONABLE, FAIR MINDED AND CHARITABLE TO ALL WE COME INTO CONTACT WITH.

notes...

day 39

PRETZEL BARK

INGREDIENTS

8 OZ PRETZELS, SLIGHTLY CRUSHED

1 C BUTTER

1 C BROWN SUGAR

2 C CHOCOLATE CHIPS

DIRECTIONS

HEAT OVEN TO 375 DEGREES.

PLACE PARCHMENT PAPER ON A 9X13 BAKING DISH, COVER WITH PRETZELS.

IN A MEDIUM SAUCE PAN, MELT BUTTER AND ADD BROWN SUGAR OVER MEDIUM HEAT, STIRRING CONSTANTLY. BRING TO A BOIL. STOP STIRRING AND LET IT BUBBLE FOR ABOUT 3 MINUTES. POUR OVER PRETZELS ON BAKING DISH AND BAKE 10 MINUTES.

SPRINKLE CHOCOLATE CHIPS OVER THE PRETZEL/TOFFEE MIXTURE. AS THE CHOCOLATE MELTS, SPREAD EVENLY WITH SPATULA.

PLACE IN REFRIGERATOR TO COOL. BREAK OFF PIECES TO SERVE.

"But you, man of God, flee from all this, and pursue righteousness, godliness, faith, love, endurance and gentleness. Fight the good fight of the faith."
- 1 Timothy 6:11-12

PAUL'S CHARGE TO TIMOTHY IS A FIERCE ONE. HE USES ACTIVE, FORCEFUL VERBS TO DESCRIBE WHAT THE CHRISTIAN LIFE MUST LOOK LIKE. IF WE ARE TO "PURSUE RIGHTEOUSNESS, GODLINESS, FAITH, LOVE, ENDURANCE AND GENTLENESS" WE MUST FLEE, PURSUE, FIGHT AND TAKE HOLD OF ALL THAT WE HAVE BEEN TAUGHT. OUR FAITH CAN'T BE PASSIVE AS THESE QUALITIES WON'T JUST APPEAR MAGICALLY IN OUR LIVES. ONLY BY HAVING AN ACTIVE FAITH AND PURSUING AND FIGHTING FOR THESE WILL OUR CHRISTIAN WALK BE CHARACTERIZED BY THESE QUALITIES.

notes...

day 40

APPLE TART

INGREDIENTS

1 1/2 C BUTTER, SOFT

1 1/2 C SUGAR

4 C FLOUR

7 GRANNY SMITH APPLES, PEELED, CORED AND THINLY SLICED

1 LEMON, JUICED

2 TSP CINNAMON

1/2 C SUGAR

1 EGG, BEATEN

DIRECTIONS

HEAT OVEN TO 350 DEGREES. GREASE A 9X13 BAKING DISH.

IN A MIXING BOWL, CREAM THE BUTTER AND SUGAR TOGETHER FOR 3 MINUTES. FOLD THE FLOUR INTO THE BUTTER/SUGAR MIX UNTIL COMPLETELY MIXED.

TAKE 2/3 OF THE DOUGH, AND PRESS DOUGH TO COVER THE BOTTOM AND THE SIDES OF THE PREPARED 9X13 BAKING DISH.

COMBINE THE PREPARED APPLES WITH THE LEMON JUICE, CINNAMON AND SUGAR AND PLACE ON TOP OF THE DOUGH.

ROLL OUT THE REST OF THE DOUGH TO ABOUT 1/4 INCH THICK. USING A PIZZA CUTTER, MAKE LATTICE STRIPS 1/2 INCH WIDE. PLACE OVER THE APPLES TO FORM LATTICE. BRUSH WITH EGG. BAKE 1 HOUR AND 15 MINUTES UNTIL GOLDEN BROWN.

"The Lord bless you and keep you; the Lord make His face shine upon you and be gracious to you; the Lord turn His face toward you and give you peace."
- Numbers 6:24-26

AS THIS JOURNEY WITH NOURISH COMES TO A CLOSE, I THOUGHT IT WAS FITTING TO END WITH NUMBERS 6:24-26. AS A TEAM, WE DO ASK THAT GOD WILL "BLESS YOU AND KEEP YOU AND MAKE HIS FACE SHINE UPON YOU". IN ASKING GOD TO BLESS OTHERS WE ARE ASKING THAT HE BLESS AND KEEP YOU, HAVE MERCY AND COMPASSION ON YOU AND GIVE APPROVAL AND PEACE. IN OFFERING A BLESSING WE ARE NOT ONLY ASKING FOR GOD'S DIVINE FAVOR TO REST UPON OTHERS, BUT WE ARE ALSO DEMONSTRATING LOVE, ENCOURAGEMENT AND A MODEL OF CARING. THANK YOU FOR TRAVELING ALONG THIS JOURNEY WITH US. OUR HOPE IS THAT YOU HAVE FOUND NOURISHMENT FOR YOUR BODY AND YOUR SOUL.

notes...

_____
_____
_____
_____
_____
_____
_____
_____

gingerbread gift tag

INGREDIENTS

1/2 C BUTTER, ROOM TEMPERATURE

1/2 CUP DARK BROWN SUGAR

1 LARGE EGG

1/3 CUP MOLASSES

2 TSP VANILLA

3 CUPS ALL-PURPOSE FLOUR

2 TSP GROUND GINGER

1 TSP GROUND CINNAMON

1/2 TSP GROUND CLOVES

RIBBON

DIRECTIONS

HEAT THE OVEN TO 375 DEGREES.

IN A BOWL WITH A MIXER, CREAM THE BUTTER AND SUGAR UNTIL THEY COME TOGETHER, ABOUT 5 MINUTES. ADD THE EGG, AND MIX. ADD THE MOLASSES AND VANILLA. MIX UNTIL COMBINED.

ADD IN FLOUR, GINGER, CINNAMON, AND CLOVES.

PLACE DOUGH ON A LIGHTLY FLOURED SURFACE AND ROLL OUT TO 1/4" THICKNESS. CUT INTO DESIRED SHAPES. USE A SKEWER TO POKE A HOLE IN THE TOP OF EACH ORNAMENT.

PLACE ON A PARCHMENT LINED BAKING SHEET, AND BAKE FOR 9 MINUTES.

ONCE COOKIES ARE COOLED, CUT RIBBON OR STRING TO DESIRED LENGTH. TIE A KNOT AT THE TOP AND PLACE ON A GIFT OR ON CHRISTMAS TREE.

popcorn garland

INGREDIENTS

1 CUP POPPED POPCORN FOR EVERY 2-3 FEET OF GARLAND

THREAD OR STRING

NEEDLE

CRANBERRY, OPTIONAL

DIRECTIONS

POP THE POPCORN AND ALLOW TO SIT FOR 24-48 HOURS TO GET STALE. THIS HELPS SO THE POPCORN DOES NOT BREAK WHEN THREADING IT.

GET THREAD (OR STRING) AND CUT TO YOUR DESIRED LENGTH. THREAD THE NEEDLE. TAKE A PIECE OF POPCORN AND STICK NEEDLE INTO THE KERNEL AREA OF THE POPCORN. PUSH THE POPCORN TO THE BOTTOM OF STRING. REPEAT PROCESS. IF YOU WANT TO ADD A CRANBERRY, ADD ONE AFTER EVERY 5 PIECES OF POPCORN.

FILL THE STRING WITH POPCORN. ONCE FINISHED TIE A KNOT ON EACH END.

REPEAT THE PROCESS UNTIL YOU GET THE NUMBER OF POPCORN GARLANDS DESIRED.

salt dough ornaments

INGREDIENTS

4 C FLOUR
1 C SALT
1 1/2 C WATER
STRING OR RIBBON
ACRYLIC PAINT, OPTIONAL
SKEWER

DIRECTIONS

HEAT OVEN TO 250 DEGREES.

MIX FLOUR, SALT AND WATER TOGETHER IN LARGE BOWL.

KNEAD UNTIL THE DOUGH IS SOFT AND MIXED TOGETHER, ABOUT 5-10 MINUTES. CUT DOUGH INTO 3 PIECES. ROLL OUT EACH PIECE OF DOUGH TO ABOUT 1/4 INCH THICK. CUT INTO DESIRED COOKIE CUTTER SHAPES. TRANSFER TO A PARCHMENT LINED SHEET TRAY. NEXT, GRAB A SKEWER AND POKE A HOLE IN THE TOP OF EACH ORNAMENT.

BAKE FOR 1-2 HOURS, OR UNTIL THE ORNAMENTS LOOK AND FEEL COMPLETELY DRY.

IF DESIRED, PAINT YOUR ORNAMENT ANY COLOR. STRING RIBBON OR STRING THROUGH TOP OF ORNAMENT AND HANG!

dried orange garland

INGREDIENTS

4-6 LARGE ORANGES

PARCHMENT PAPER

FISHING WIRE OR THREAD

LARGE NEEDLE

DIRECTIONS

HEAT THE OVEN TO 225 DEGREES. GET 2 TO 3 SHEET TRAYS AND LINE THEM WITH PARCHMENT PAPER. SLICE ORANGES ABOUT 1/8 TO 1/4 INCH THICK. LAY SLICES ON SHEET TRAY. BLOT THEM WITH A PAPER TOWEL TO DRY OUT THE MOISTURE.

PLACE IN OVEN FOR AN HOUR AND A HALF. TURN ORANGES OVER AND COOK AN ADDITIONAL HOUR AND A HALF (A TOTAL OF 3 HOURS OF COOKING). ORANGES SHOULD BE LIGHTLY BROWNED.

ONCE FINISHED COOKING, LET ORANGES AIR DRY, ABOUT 2 HOURS. GET FISHING LINE OR THREAD (IF YOU USE THREAD GRAB A NEEDLE TO HELP POKE THROUGH THE DRIED ORANGE). NEXT, THREAD THROUGH FLESH OF THE ORANGE NOT THE RIND. SPACE THEM OUT HOWEVER YOU DESIRE, WE PREFER THEM TO HAVE A 2 INCH GAP IN BETWEEN ORANGES.

a big thank you to...

EACH OF OUR HUSBANDS FOR ENCOURAGEMENT:
KYLE POTTS, PAUL BAXLEY, CODY BRAZEAL

OUR CREATIVE TEAM:
DAKOTA, NATALIE, & CHELSEA

BECKHAM, HARRISON & DUKE FOR BEING OUR HELPERS & TASTE TESTERS
CREATIVE TILE FOR YOUR TILE WE USED AS BACKDROPS
CHELSEA & CHRIS CUMIFORD FOR YOUR BEAUTIFUL HOME
PACIFIC TREASURES FOR YOUR BEAUTIFUL DISHES
JILL BRAZEAL & MADDIE SULLIVAN FOR ALL YOUR HELP
QUALITY MEATS FOR YOUR MEAT
VISALIA FARMERS MARKET FOR FRESH VEGGIES
FRIENDS & FAMILY FOR ALL YOUR SUPPORT!

merry christmas!